The
Children
are Free

The Children are Free

Reexamining the Biblical Evidence on Same-sex Relationships

Rev. Jeff Miner and John Tyler Connoley

Jesus Metropolitan Community Church
Indianapolis, Indiana

ISBN-13:   978-0-9719296-0-9
ISBN-10:   0-9719296-0-2

For more information, contact:
Jesus Metropolitan Community Church
2950 East 55th Place
Indianapolis, Indiana 46220
(317) 722-0000
www.jesusmcc.org

Dedication

Jeff dedicates this book to the countless homosexual Christians of the past who lived difficult lives of struggle and denial because they believed that was what God wanted of them. May God give them a special place in heaven.

Tyler dedicates this book to his father and mother, who taught him to love Jesus and think for himself, and to all other Christian parents of gay, lesbian, and bisexual children. May they find peace and hope for their children in the words of this book.

Acknowledgements

We are deeply grateful to Jeramy Townsley, who generously shared important research, and to David Squire, Administrator at Jesus MCC, who coordinated production of this book.

We would also like to thank Christine Larson, research librarian at Earlham College's Lilly Library, and the other library staff who helped locate many of the sources used in this book.

Thank you also to the many people who read drafts of this work, offering comments and criticisms, particularly Deb Doty. Deb, God brought you along just when we needed you.

Finally, thanks go to Maggie, without whom we might still be searching for a title.

In Memoriam

Funds for the publication of this book were provided by the Miller–Rushton Liberty Fund at Jesus Metropolitan Community Church, endowed by the Joseph F. Miller Foundation, in loving memory of Ken Rushton.

Ken Rushton grew up in Indianapolis, Indiana, the son of fundamentalist Christian parents. His family attended a prominent Baptist church, where in 1973 Ken graduated as valedictorian of the church-run high school and then began working for the church. Church and faith were at the center of Ken Rushton's life.

But Ken also realized he was gay. Soon after graduation, he "came out" and found a partner, Joe Miller. When, a few years later, word leaked back to his church, friends there promptly cut all ties — including the church's pastor and his son, both of whom had been among Ken's closest friends. There was no dialogue, no prayers, no expressions of concern; he was simply cut off. Feeling he was living under condemnation, Ken prayed often and earnestly for God to change him — to take away his homosexuality.

Rejected by his church, Ken drifted from his faith, moved away, eventually began using drugs, and, several years ago, took his own life.

Ken's story is typical of millions of gay and lesbian people whose churches have, however well intentioned, sentenced them to life without hope. May this book make a difference for all who struggle as Ken did.

"Blessed are those who mourn, for they will be comforted."
Matthew 5:4.

About the Authors

Jeff Miner is the pastor of Jesus Metropolitan Community Church in Indianapolis, Indiana. He was raised in fundamentalist independent Baptist churches, and received his undergraduate degree from Bob Jones University. In college, Jeff felt called to the ministry, but deferred that calling while trying to come to terms with being gay. In the meantime, he attended Harvard Law School, graduating with honors in 1983. Several years later, after intensive study of the Bible and homosexuality, Jeff came to peace with being gay. Soon he discovered the Metropolitan Community Churches, a Christian denomination that has arisen out of the gay, lesbian, bisexual, and transgender community. There, Jeff realized he could fulfill his call to ministry. He completed his clergy training and was ordained in 1997.

Before his ordination, Jeff worked as an attorney for 13 years, last serving as a Deputy Chief Council for a federal banking agency.

Jeff lives with his spouse, David Zier. They were joined in Holy Union on September 8, 1990, and live in Indianapolis.

John Tyler Connoley is the son of Wesleyan missionaries. He spent most of his childhood years in Zambia, Africa, and has lived in Korea, the Philippines, and all of the West Coast states.

He came out to himself in 1991, while attending Indiana Wesleyan University, and has since sought to live a life that integrates his deep faith in God with his sexuality. While working on this book, Tyler completed his M.A. in Biblical Studies at Earlham School of Religion in Richmond, Indiana.

He is married to Rob Connoley.

Contents

Special Note

Some readers may wonder why this book does not address what the Bible says about transgenderism. The questions transgender people bring to Scripture require and deserve a separate, full analysis, and lie beyond the scope of this book.

Preface

When we began this project, we thought our goal should be to create an intermediate size booklet — something in-between the large books and small pamphlets which are currently available on the subject of the Bible and homosexuality. However, as we began doing our research, we were frustrated that many books on this subject rely too much on speculation and contain little documentation. We also found no one work that covers *all* the biblical texts (both the "clobber passages" and the affirming passages). Thus, our goal evolved from writing a simple summary to seeking to prepare a comprehensive, well-documented analysis of all the biblical data on homosexuality.

We hold the Scriptures in highest esteem, and offer this book to others who care passionately about what the Bible says on this subject. We are especially excited to present the results of recent scholarship on Jesus' encounter with a Roman centurion (Matthew 10) and various biblical references to eunuchs. Endnotes have been included at the end of each chapter for those who wish to take their study further.

In this book, we have limited ourselves to a single question: *Can two people of the same sex live in committed, loving relationship with the blessing of God?* We believe this is the question most commonly asked by gay, lesbian, and bisexual Christians today.

All we ask of any reader is that you give us a fair hearing. We invite you to pray this prayer: "God, if this book contains truth, help me to recognize it." Our prayer is that God will use this book to bring peace to many homosexuals who have struggled, to their loved ones who worry about them, and to others wrestling with how their church should respond to homosexuals. May the grace of our Lord Jesus Christ be with you all.

Chapter One

The Clobber Passages

Can two people of the same sex live in committed, loving relationship with the blessing of God?

As we begin to grapple with this question, in this first chapter we examine what are often referred to as the "clobber passages." These are the handful of Bible passages that some Christians use to "clobber" gay, lesbian, and bisexual people. As we show in later chapters, *there are also many wonderful, powerful Bible passages that affirm gay people*, but for some it is not possible to accept that God affirms them until they have first worked through the clobber passages. So, although this may seem like a difficult starting point, we believe it is important to study these passages before moving to the gay-positive passages.

Are there really only six?

If you flipped through this chapter before reading it, you might have been surprised at how few Scriptures are covered. Given how often some Christians preach against homosexuality, you would think there must be hundreds of Scriptures on the subject. In fact there are only six traditional clobber passages and, as we will show, none of them speaks to the situation of twenty-first century gay people who desire to live in loving relationships with the blessing of God. By contrast, there are literally hundreds of passages that regulate every aspect of heterosexuality. As lesbian comedian Lynn Lavner likes to say, "It isn't that God doesn't love the heterosexuals as much as God loves us, it's just that they require a good bit more supervision." (Hopefully you haven't lost your sense of humor in your search for truth!)

You also might have noticed the absence of clobber passages in the Gospels (Matthew, Mark, Luke, and John). Although Jesus said many things that apply to the lives of twenty-first century gay people, we have no indication that Jesus ever said anything negative on the subject of homosexuality. In fact, the opposite is true. When Jesus met a gay man, his response was very affirming. But we will save that for Chapter Two. To begin, let's look at each of the six passages commonly used against gay, lesbian, and bisexual people.

Sodom and Gomorrah (Genesis 19)

We begin with the best known of the six passages — the story of Sodom and Gomorrah. This story is told in one of the oldest books in the Bible, and has been a favorite among artists and writers for centuries. Even if you have never read the Old Testament account of the destruction of Sodom and Gomorrah, you have probably seen it portrayed in a movie or book. Since the biblical account is very long, we will paraphrase it here. You can find the original in Genesis 19 and the preceding chapters.

Abraham had a nephew named Lot who moved to Sodom. At the time, Sodom was considered a comfortable, modern, sophisticated city, and Lot thought it would be a better place to raise his family than out on the plains with Abraham, who was a nomad. Unfortunately, the city was also full of wickedness, and God told Abraham that it would soon be destroyed. Two angels were sent to assess the situation in Sodom, and when Lot saw them in the town square, he invited them to his house for dinner and lodging. He did not recognize they were angels. He seems, however, to have felt a responsibility to be hospitable to strangers — perhaps because he remembered having been a stranger himself.

That night, when the city dwellers learned Lot had welcomed two strangers into his house and into their city, all the people gathered at his door. They demanded that Lot deliver the two men to them so they might "know them." (Genesis 19:5) (The Hebrew word translated "know" in this passage is sometimes used in Scripture to mean sexual intercourse, and given the context of the passage, that is probably what it means here.[1]) Lot pleaded with his neighbors not to do such an evil thing. In a despicable act, he even offered them his virgin daughters instead, but the men persisted. Finally, the angels struck all those outside with blindness and warned Lot and his family they should leave the city because God would soon destroy it for its wickedness. The very next day, fire came down from heaven and destroyed the city and all its inhabitants.

Since the Middle Ages, many Christian theologians have viewed this story as a blanket condemnation of homosexuality. They have perpetuated the idea that Sodom was destroyed for its sexual wickedness and that the proof of this wickedness was the desire of the men of Sodom to have homosexual sex. Let's test this interpretation against both the facts relayed in Genesis 19 and the interpretation of the story by later authors of the Bible. First, let's examine the facts.

The text of the story tells us that "the men of Sodom, both young and old, all the people to the last man" (vs. 4) gathered at Lot's door and demanded that his guests be brought out to them. This language is important because it makes clear that the group at Lot's door was comprised of either all the people of the city (men and women) or, at a minimum, all the males of the city, both boys and men. This is a telling fact.

Today, San Francisco has the reputation for being the "gayest" city in the world. Yet even in San Francisco, gay men constitute far less than half the total male population. If the Scripture text had told us that "certain men of Sodom" or even "many men of Sodom" gathered at the door, we might then surmise that the men at the door could have been motivated by homosexual desire. But the text says "both young and old, all the people to the last man" gathered at the door. To suggest that every man and boy in Sodom was homosexual is simply not credible. Any reasonable interpretation of the story must account for the fact that all the males of Sodom (both homosexual and heterosexual), and perhaps even the women, participated in this attack. Something other than homosexual desire seems to have been at work here.

This point is reinforced by another fact recounted in the story. We are told that Lot, in a last-ditch effort to save his guests, offered his virgin daughters to the men at the door. Although Lot's offer is reprehensible, it does yield another important interpretive clue. Suppose you were hosting a dinner party, when suddenly a group of men that you knew to be homosexual began angrily beating on the door, demanding that you send out a male guest from your house. Would it make any sense to offer them a beautiful woman instead? Of course not! If the men were motivated by homosexual desire, offering them heterosexual sex instead would be nonsensical. Lot knew the men of Sodom much better than any of today's fundamentalist preachers do. And it's obvious he believed the crowd outside his door was predominantly heterosexual. Why else would he offer his daughters?

Although it might be simpler to blame what took place in Genesis 19 on homosexuals, the facts indicate that something far more encompassing and complex was taking place. But what? If the motivation for the attack was not homosexual desire, then what was it?

Consider an example from modern times. On August 9, 1997 in New York City, two white police officers were strip-searching a black Haitian immigrant named Abner Louima and grew angry with him. They dragged him into a bathroom and, while one officer held him down, the other repeatedly rammed a broken broom up Louima's rectum. While they did this, the officers reportedly yelled things like, "We're gonna teach you n****rs to respect police officers!"[2] In the aftermath of this terrible incident, nobody has suggested the assault was motivated by homosexual desire. Intuitively, we recognize the two officers were motivated by hatred and fear of people like Abner Louima. In their minds, there was no better way to demean and humiliate an "enemy" than to sexually violate him.

4

This same evil motivation is behind the vulgar phrase "F**k you!" That's why, when Tyler is poking along the highway in his '87 Honda Civic and an angry man in a Ford F150 flies by and flips him the finger, Tyler doesn't think, "Oh, he must think I'm cute!" Tyler knows the man is angry — maybe angry enough to brutalize him.

From archeological records, we know it was also a common practice in the Near East during ancient times for soldiers to use homosexual rape as a way of humiliating their enemies.[3] When victorious soldiers wanted to break the spirit of their defeated enemies, they would "treat them like women" by raping them. The practice was not driven by sexual desire, but by brutality and hatred toward the enemy.

The motivation to sexually abuse those we hate is, sadly, part of the general human experience (even if it is not part of each of our personal experiences). And it is this motivation, not homosexual desire, which stands behind the sin of Sodom. Perhaps the men of that city feared the two angelic strangers were spies. Perhaps the fact that Lot (a recent immigrant) had taken them in served to heighten their suspicion. Whatever caused their panic, a mob mentality took over, and before long the people of Sodom were at Lot's house clamoring to brutalize the strangers. This is a story about attempted mob violence, not homosexual desire.

To test this proposition, let's ask a simple question. Suppose the two angels in the story had been women, but the story otherwise unfolded exactly the same: The men of Sodom clamored to have sex with the two female angels and God destroyed the city. Do you think anyone would conclude this story was a blanket condemnation of heterosexuality? Of course not! Instead, we all would conclude (correctly) that the wickedness of Sodom was shown by their desire to sexually violate two strangers in their midst.

In fact, this is the way other authors of the Bible interpreted this story.[4] There are about twenty references to the story of Sodom in the Bible, and *none of them says homosexuality was the sin of Sodom.* One of the most extensive references to Sodom is found in Ezekiel, which says, "This was the guilt of your sister Sodom: She and her daughters had pride, excess of food, and prosperous ease, but did not aid the poor and needy. They were haughty and did abominable things before me; therefore I removed them when I saw it." (Ezekiel 16:49-50[5]) It is clear from this passage (and others like it[6]) that the abomination of Sodom, according to the Old Testament prophets, was that they behaved with callous indifference toward the weak and vulnerable — the poor, orphans, widows, and strangers in their midst.

Why then do some Christians interpret this story as condemning all homosexual behavior? We would submit that their interpretation is driven by anti-gay prejudice. Many Christians only know the stereotypes they learned in childhood. They buy into the idea that all gay men are predators and that loving relationships between inherently homosexual people do not exist. So they read the story of Sodom and see a stereotype of what they think all gay people are like. They then assume the story must be a sweeping condemnation of homosexuality, because they assume all homosexuality takes the form shown in this story. In truth, this story is at most a condemnation of homosexual rape. And, as other Scriptures affirm, it is more generally a condemnation of the mistreatment of those who are most vulnerable, including strangers. It is ironic that the story of Sodom is now used by Christians to justify hatred toward another vulnerable group — gay people.

This story clearly does not apply to the question we bring to Scripture, namely, whether two persons of the same sex can live in a loving, committed relationship with the blessing of God. So we can take the first clobber passage and set it aside.

Going after strange flesh (Jude 7)

The second of the clobber passages is another reference to Sodom and Gomorrah. In the King James Version of the Bible it reads:

> "Sodom and Gomorrah, and the cities about them in like manner, giving themselves over to fornication, and going

after strange flesh, are set forth for an example, suffering the vengeance of eternal fire." (Jude 7[7])

When we read this verse in modern America, having been raised in a culture that despises gays and refers to them as "queer," it is easy to assume Jude's reference to "going after strange flesh" must mean homosexuality. For many heterosexual people, it seems unnatural or strange for a person to desire intimacy with someone of the same sex. However, well-informed theologians will tell you this is not what Jude was talking about.

At the time the book of Jude was written, many believed some of the women of Sodom had engaged in intercourse with male angels. This belief was probably derived from Genesis 6:1, 2 and 4, where we are told the "Sons of God"(angels) took the daughters of humans as wives. This was the final act which brought God's judgment on the earth in the form of a great flood. And it seems some Jewish writers believed this was also the sin which sealed Sodom's fate. According to first century legend, some of the women of Sodom (and other wicked ancient cities) were thought to have had sex with beings who were made of different flesh — angelic flesh.[8] This is what Jude was referring to when he talked about "going after strange flesh." He was referring to heterosexual sex between male angels and human women, not homosexual sex between humans. Many theologians, including many conservatives, interpret the passage this way.[9]

Again we ask, does this passage apply to the question we bring to Scripture? And we must answer that it has nothing to say about whether it is possible for two humans of the same sex to have an intimate, loving relationship with the blessing of God. We can, therefore, set aside clobber passage number two.

How language is interpreted

Before delving into the next several clobber passages, it will be helpful to pause briefly to remind ourselves of some basic, common-sense rules for understanding and interpreting human language.

Perhaps it will help to draw an analogy from Jeff's thirteen years of experience as a lawyer. (Don't worry, this won't be too dry.)

When the Supreme Court (or any other court) issues a written decision, the first question any good lawyer asks is: "What is the *holding* of the case?" The term "holding" refers to the rule established by the court's decision. Once this question is answered, we know what the case means, right?

Wrong! Every good lawyer knows that to stop the analysis after figuring out what rule the court established would constitute gross malpractice. There is a vital follow-up question that must be asked: "What were the facts of the case?"

This second question is essential because judges and lawyers have learned through experience that you cannot truly understand a rule unless you also understand the context in which the rule was issued. Because of this, one of the first principles drilled into the head of every law student is that judicial holdings are *limited to the facts of the case.* In other words, you cannot take a rule that a judge issued in one context and automatically apply it to a different set of facts. Before this can be done, the facts of both cases must be carefully examined to determine whether they are similar enough for the rule to apply to both cases.

This methodology is not unique to lawyers. It is based on common sense and the way we use language in the ordinary ebb and flow of life. For example, suppose a married couple is talking and the wife says to her husband: "Don't touch me." She has announced a "rule." Now, suppose someone copies down this statement and hands it to us, saying, "These were her exact words." We now have the wife's words in front of us in black and white, and that is all we need to interpret the meaning of her statement accurately, right?

Wrong! Until we know the context in which her statement was made, there is every possibility we will completely misunderstand and misapply what she said. For example, if the woman made this statement in the context of an angry encounter with her husband during a bitter divorce, then her statement can fairly be interpreted as an absolute command that her husband should never again touch her under any circumstances. On the other hand, if she made this statement when she was happily married, but lying in bed sick with a fever and her skin was prickly, her statement has a radically different meaning.

This simple example reminds us of a very important principle: If we want to interpret spoken or written statements accurately, we must carefully study the context in which the statements were made. Otherwise we can completely misunderstand what was intended.

Theologians of all stripes (including the most fundamentalist) have long followed this rule when interpreting statements found in the Bible. As Jeff's fundamentalist Baptist preachers and professors used to say over and over again, "A text taken out of context is pretext."

We are used to applying this principle in many biblical settings. For example, in 1 Corinthians chapter 11, the Apostle Paul says women should wear a veil when praying. He also says they should have long hair. Here are two rather simple, straightforward rules announced in the New Testament. How should we interpret them?

Some Christians have tried to interpret them without any reference to the cultural context in which the Apostle Paul spoke. So they require their women to wear hats in church (a modern type of veil) and require them to maintain hair that is shoulder length or longer.

But others who have studied the cultural context of this passage tell us that in Paul's time only prostitutes wore short hair and appeared in public unveiled.[10] If this is true, then the likely meaning of Paul's ruling changes radically from an absolute command to one that was meant to address a problem unique to the culture of the time — women who wore short hair or appeared unveiled in public could easily be mistaken for prostitutes. Today, even most conservative Christians do not require their women to wear head coverings or to keep their hair long. They take this position even though the words of the Bible specifically say women should do so. They refrain from imposing these requirements because they understand that the meaning of words is determined largely by the context in which they are spoken.

In the next few pages, we ask you to apply this same time-honored, common-sense approach to the passages commonly used to clobber homosexuals. When you do, we believe you will discover a very different meaning. Consider, for example, the rules found in Leviticus.

Do not lie with men as you would with women. (Leviticus 18:22 and 20:13)

These two verses in Leviticus read as follows in the King James Version:

"Thou shalt not lie with mankind as with womankind; it is an abomination." (Leviticus 18:22)

"If a man also lie with mankind as he lieth with a woman, both of them have committed an abomination; they shall surely be put to death; their blood be upon them." (Leviticus 20:13)

As we have seen above, if we wish to understand the true meaning of these verses, we must look at their context, both textual and historical. Until we understand what prompted these rules in Old Testament times, we will not be able to determine if the rules should be applied to the case of two people in committed, loving relationship.

The text itself gives us a big clue as to the intended meaning. Three different times we are specifically told that the rules set forth in chapters 18 and 20 are meant to prevent the Israelites from doing what the Egyptians and Canaanites did.[11] The term *Canaanites* refers to the group of nations who lived in the land into which the Israelites migrated when they left Egypt. It follows, therefore, if we can determine what type of homosexual behavior was common among the Canaanites and Egyptians, we will better understand what these verses were meant to prohibit.

Biblical historians tell us the Canaanite religions surrounding the Israelites at the time of Leviticus often included fertility rites consisting of sexual rituals. These rituals were thought to bring the blessing of the god or goddess on crop and livestock production. During the rituals, whole families, including husbands, wives, mothers, fathers, sons, daughters, cousins, aunts and uncles would sometimes have sex. Also included was sex with temple prostitutes. In short, every kind of sexual practice imaginable was performed at these rituals, including homosexual sex.[12]

Consider one specific example. Historians tell us that many Canaanites and Egyptians worshipped a goddess of love and fertility called Astarte or Ishtar. Within her temples were special priests called *assinu,* who were deemed to have special powers. Physical contact with the assinu was believed to ward off evil and promote good luck. These priests were, in effect, living good luck charms, and worshipers would often ritually touch them as part of their worship practices. Sexual intercourse was considered especially effective for gaining the goddess's favor, because the male worshiper was offering his greatest possession, semen (which was thought to be the essence of life), to the goddess through her priests. Depositing semen in the body of a priest of the goddess was believed to guarantee one's immortality. Similar cultic sexual practices flourished in connection with many other ancient pagan deities.[13]

This is what was going on in Canaan and Egypt at the time the Levitical rules were announced — homosexual temple prostitution. And as already noted, Leviticus 18 and 20 specifically say they were written to address pagan religious practices. Leviticus 18 begins with the admonition, "You shall not do as they do in the land of Egypt, where you lived, and you shall not do as they do in the land of Canaan, where I am bringing you." (18:3) Chapter 20 is even more specific, beginning with an injunction against the pagan practices associated with a god named Molech. And both chapters include long lists of sexual practices common in the cultic rituals we mentioned above. However, neither of them speaks to the question of whether

two people of the same sex can live in loving relationship with the
blessing of God.

In fact, historians tell us our model of loving, long-term homosexual relationships did not meaningfully exist in Canaanite culture.
This was a tribal culture in which it would have been virtually impossible to form such relationships. Offspring were essential to survival
in this primitive agricultural economy. Moreover, there were rigid
distinctions between women's work and men's work. If two men had
lived together as a couple, for example, one of them would have been
placed in the position of doing women's work, and the presence of a
man working among the women of the village would not have been
tolerated.[14]

It simply is not reasonable to believe the author of Leviticus
intended to prohibit a form of homosexual relationship that did not
exist at the time. When read in textual and historical context, the
prohibitions in Leviticus 18 and 20 are clearly directed at homosexual
temple prostitution, and that is how they should be applied.

Some people may object, saying, "But if you ignore the context
and just read the words of Leviticus 18:22 and 20:13 in black and
white, they appear to prohibit *all* sex between men, not just sex in
pagan rituals." But that is the whole point: The meaning of words
depends on context. Remember, the words of 1 Corinthians 11 also
appear to require long hair and head coverings for *all* women in *all*
circumstances. But, because we have studied the context, we know
that is not what was meant. *A text taken out of context is pretext.* Let's
apply the same common-sense rule here.

The Leviticus passages were clearly written in the context of
pagan religious ritual. Since we are not bringing a question about the
appropriateness of cultic sex practices for modern Christians, we can
safely set aside these clobber passages.

Trading natural relations for unnatural (Romans 1:21-28)

The next clobber passage may seem daunting when first
approached because it is written in a rhetorical style most modern

readers are not used to. Paul, the writer of Romans, was trained as a scholar of Greek classics and Hebrew literature, and his style may seem obscure to those of us (like Tyler) who enjoy reading *Dear Abby* and *USA Today*. The pertinent passage reads as follows in the King James Version:

"Because that, when they knew God, they glorified him not as God, neither were thankful; but became vain in their imaginations, and their foolish heart was darkened. Professing themselves to be wise, they became fools, and changed the glory of incorruptible God into an image made like to corruptible man, and to birds, and four-footed beasts, and creeping things. Wherefore God also gave them up to uncleanness through the lusts of their own hearts, to dishonor their own bodies between themselves: who changed the truth of God into a lie, and worshipped and served the creature more than the Creator, who is blessed forever. Amen.

"For this cause God gave them up unto vile affections: for even their women did change natural use into that which is against nature: and likewise also the men leaving the natural use of the women, burned in their lust one toward another; men with men working that which is unseemly, and receiving in themselves that recompense of their error which was meet. And even as they did not like to retain God in their knowledge, God gave them over to a reprobate mind, to do those things which are not convenient; being filled with all unrighteousness, fornication, wickedness, covetousness, maliciousness; full of envy, murder, debate, deceit, malignity; whisperers, backbiters, haters of God, despiteful, proud, boasters, inventors of evil things, disobedient to parents, without understanding, covenant breakers, without natural affection, implacable, unmerciful." (Romans 1:21-28)

Though it may come as a surprise, we consider this to be the easiest of the clobber passages to interpret. This is because Paul, in his classically trained style, thoroughly explains the factual assumptions and rationale behind his condemnation of the behavior described here. This makes it easy for us to answer our question: Does this passage apply to inherently same-gender-attracted people who are living in loving, committed relationships?

If we follow the passage, step-by-step, we find Paul is moving through a logical progression. He is talking about people who:

1. Refused to acknowledge and glorify God. (v. 21)
2. Began worshipping idols (images of created things, rather than the Creator). (v. 23)
3. Were more interested in earthly pursuits than spiritual pursuits. (v. 25)
4. Gave up their natural, *i.e.*, innate, passion for the opposite sex in an unbounded search for pleasure. (v. 26-27)
5. Lived lives full of covetousness, malice, envy, strife, slander, disrespect for parents, pride, and hatred of God. (v. 29-31)

The model of homosexual behavior Paul was addressing here is explicitly associated with idol worship (probably temple prostitution[15]), and with people who, in an unbridled search for pleasure (or because of religious rituals associated with their idolatry), broke away from their natural sexual orientation, participating in promiscuous sex with anyone available.

There are, no doubt, modern people who engage in homosexual sex for reasons similar to those identified in Romans 1. If someone began with a clear heterosexual orientation, but rejected God and began experimenting with gay sex simply as a way of experiencing a new set of pleasures, then this passage may apply to that person. But this is not the experience of the vast majority of gay, lesbian, and bisexual people. Consider Tyler's story:

> From the time Tyler was a very young man his main

desire was to do God's will. He was raised by missionary parents, and at the age of five he acknowledged his need for God and prayed for Jesus to come into his heart. He didn't understand exactly what that meant, but he always tried to live a life that glorified God. In high school, his friends thought of him as different because his faith in God and in the teachings of his church did not allow him to drink and dance. When a girl asked him to the prom, he went, but he made sure they started the date by praying together. Unlike the people condemned in Romans 1, Tyler acknowledged, glorified, and worshipped God. For him, spiritual pursuits were much more important than earthly pleasures.

However, by the time Tyler decided to go to a Christian college, he was already having feelings of attraction toward men and knew he was not attracted to women. He believed these feelings were wrong, so he suppressed his natural attractions and told himself he must be asexual. And, when he finally acknowledged his attraction to men during his fourth year of college, it was not during a search for unbounded sexual pleasure or in the context of pagan worship rituals. It was during a night of intense prayer when he was questioning whether he should try to pursue a relationship with a female friend. During that time of prayer, Tyler was strongly impressed that he needed, instead, to deal with his innate attraction to men.

For Tyler, a Christian child of missionaries, his first reaction was to seek spiritual advice. He immediately went to a trusted professor and soon began therapy with one of the counselors at his Christian school. For the next several years, he continued to remain celibate as he wrestled with Scripture and with his church's teachings, trying to find out how he should live as a gay man. He tried always to live a life free of covetousness, malice, envy, strife, and pride. And, even when Tyler came to the conclusion that Scripture affirmed him as an innately gay individual, his respect for the teaching of his parents and his love of God convinced him to remain a virgin until meeting his spouse, Rob.

Jeff's story is similar. And we know of hundreds of other gay people who could tell stories of struggling with their same-sex attractions while diligently serving God. These are not idolaters, people who hated God and pursued their own desire for new and greater sexual thrills. These are lovers of God who, nevertheless, have been attracted to people of the same sex from early in life. They are innate (*i.e.*, natural) homosexuals.

Paul simply does not address our model of stable, loving homosexual relationships among people of faith. It might be fair to ask, "If Paul had known some people are innately homosexual and if he had been aware of stable, loving gay relationships among devout people of faith, would he still have disapproved?" However, any answer we came up with would be fanciful speculation, because the fact is Paul did not address this issue in his letter to the Romans. He was addressing a different set of facts and, under the guidance of the Holy Spirit, issued a ruling applicable to those facts. We must look elsewhere in Scripture for guidance on our question.

No fems? No fairies? (1 Corinthians 6:9-10 and 1 Timothy 1:10)

A final passage of Scripture often used against gay people is 1 Corinthians 6:9-10, which reads as follows in the King James Version:

> "Know ye not that the unrighteous shall not inherit the kingdom of God? Be not deceived, neither fornicators, nor idolaters, nor adulterers, nor effeminate, nor abusers of themselves with mankind, nor thieves . . . shall inherit the kingdom of God."

In this passage there are two key phrases relevant to our discussion. First there is the reference to "effeminate" persons, which is often viewed as a reference to nelly gay men. In truth, however, the Greek word translated "effeminate" in verse 9 is quite broad. The word is *malakoi*, and it literally means "soft."[16] So Paul is saying "soft people" will not inherit the kingdom of God. Since we know Paul was not talking about the Pillsbury Dough Boy, we have to ask what he meant. This common Greek word had different connotations depending on the context in which it was used. In terms of morality, it generally referred to something like *laziness, degeneracy, decadence, or lack of courage.*[17] The connotation was of being "soft like a woman" or like the delicate expensive fabrics worn by rich men. In the patriarchal culture of the time, women were thought to be weaker than men, more fearful, more vulnerable, and more vain. Thus, men who ate too much, liked expensive things, were lazy, or liked to dress well were considered "soft like a woman." Although this type of misogynistic thinking is intolerable in our modern society, it was common in ancient times and explains why the King James Version translated *malakoi* as "effeminate."

But it is important to understand the difference between ancient and modern notions of what makes one effeminate. Paul wasn't condemning men who swish and carry purses; he was condemning a type of moral weakness. The ancient Roman and Greek understanding of what it meant to be manly or womanly was quite different from today. First-century Romans didn't think of effeminacy as merely a homosexual trait. In that culture, any man who was more interested in pleasure than in duty was considered to be woman-like. And men who worked to make themselves more attractive, "whether they were trying to attract men or women, were called effeminate."[18] They saw all pleasure-seeking men as effeminate, whomever they sought pleasure with. In first-century Roman terms, most pro-wrestlers in the WWF (manly men by our definitions) would be considered effeminate, because of their apparent interest in fancy, hyper-masculine costumes and posturing. From this perspective, Paul was condemning men who are vain, fearful, and self-indulgent.

In recent years, however, some have suggested that, in the context in which it appears in 1 Corinthians 6, *malakoi* may refer specifically to male prostitutes, who would have served as the receptive partner (*i.e.*, soft, "woman-like") in sexual intercourse. This translation is reflected in two of the most widely used modern English translations of the Bible, the New International Version and the New Revised Standard Version. Since *malakoi* was used to refer to men who exhibited the negative traits associated with women in first-century culture, it's not hard to see how the term might also be used to refer to male prostitutes. They would be viewed as sexually indulgent (a trait associated with women) and as the ones who played a receptive role in intercourse (again, associated with women). Because here Paul uses *malakoi* in a list of sexual sins, it is possible to infer that he may have been referring specifically to male prostitutes, rather than soft men in general.

However, regardless of whether Paul intended to refer specifically to male prostitutes or more generally to all men considered morally soft, it is apparent that the term *malakoi* has nothing to do with the question we bring to Scripture. We are not defending prostitution, nor vanity or self-indulgence. Our question is whether same-sex couples may live in loving, committed relationships with the blessing of God. The term *malakoi* does not address that.

The next key phrase in this passage is rendered in the King James Version as "abusers of themselves with mankind." A similar phrase appears in a list of sins in I Timothy 1:10. Both phrases are derived from a single Greek word, *arsenokoitai*, which is quite rare. In fact, these two biblical references may be the first examples we have of this word being used in the literature of the time.[19] Because the word is so rare, its exact meaning is probably lost forever. However, some scholars have worked hard to make an educated guess.

One translation technique is to look at the root words alone. *Arsenokoitai* is a combination of two existing words, one meaning "bed" and referring to sex, and another meaning "male."[20] Thus, some scholars surmise the term has something to do with male sexual expression — perhaps exclusive male sexual expression, since no woman is mentioned.

Unfortunately, this method of translation often leads people astray. For example, imagine a future translator coming across the word "lady-killer" two thousand years from now and wanting to know what it means. It's clear the phrase is made from two words, lady and killer. So, it must mean a woman who kills, right? Or is it a person who kills ladies? The difficulty in obtaining a good translation is clear — particularly when we know lady-killer was a term used in the 1970s to refer to men whom women supposedly found irresistible.[21]

A better way to understand what Paul may have meant by *arsenokoitai* is to look for other instances of the word in the subsequent writings of his time. This approach yields several telling facts. First, two early church writers who dealt with the subject of homosexual behavior extensively, Clement of Alexandria and John Chrysostom, never used the word in their discussions of same-sex behavior. The word shows up in their writing, but only in places where they appear to be quoting the list of sins found in 1 Corinthians 6, not in places where they discuss homosexuality. This suggests they did not believe Paul's term referred to homosexual behavior.[22]

A similar pattern is found in other writings of the time. There are hundreds of Greek writings from this period that refer to homosexual activity using terms other than *arsenokoitai.*[23] If Paul had intended to refer generally to homosexual sex, or to one of the partners in gay-male sex, he had other commonly-used, well-known words at his disposal. He wouldn't have had to resort to this ambiguous compound word, which future generations would find difficult to translate. Apparently Paul was trying to refer to some more obscure type of behavior.

This conclusion is reinforced by a survey of the actual uses of *arsenokoitai* in Greek literature. Scholars have identified only 73 times this term is used in the six centuries after Paul.[24] (There are no known instances before Paul.) In virtually every instance the term appears in a list of sins (like Paul's) without any story line or other context to shed light on its meaning. There are, however, a few helpful exceptions. In one instance, a Greek author uses the term when cataloguing the sins of the Greek gods.[25] In this context, the term is probably intended to refer to the time Zeus abducted and raped a young boy, Ganymede. *Arsenokoitai* is also used in an ancient legend in which the snake in the Garden of Eden is said to have become a Satanic figure named Naas. Naas uses a variety of means (including sleeping with both Adam and Eve) to gain power over and destroy them. In this story, Naas is said to have gone to Adam and had him like a boy. Naas' sin is called *arsenokoitai*.[26] These examples suggest that *arsenokoitai* refers to instances when one male uses his superior power or position to take sexual advantage of another.

This premise is reinforced by yet another translation technique. As noted above, most of the times when *arsenokoitai* is used in early Greek literature, it occurs in a list of sins (just like in 1 Corinthians 6).[27] Common experience tells us list-makers tend to group similar items together. (When Tyler makes a grocery list, he puts the vegetables at the top, the dairy at the bottom, and everything else in-between.) In these lists, *arsenokoitai* is often placed at the end of the list of sex sins and the beginning of the list of economic sins or vice versa.[28] For example, in 1 Corinthians 6, we find it between *malakoi* (which may refer to male prostitutes) and "thieves." In I Timothy 1:10, the word appears between "fornication" and "slave traders." This is consistent with the meaning suggested above — that *arsenokoitai* describes a male who aggressively takes sexual advantage of another male. Examples of this type of behavior would include a man who rapes another (as in the Sodom story or the story of Zeus and Ganymede) or a man who uses economic power to buy sex from a male prostitute who sells his body to survive. This latter example is an especially neat fit if *malakoi* is understood to be a reference to the prostitute, in which case Paul's list would include a reference both to the male prostitute (*malakoi*) and the man who takes advantage of the prostitute (*arsenokoitai*). This type of person is a close kin to the thief and the greedy — the two Greek words that most often follow *arsenokoitai* in the lists of sins.

A thief, a greedy person, and one who uses power to obtain sex are all seizing something that does not rightfully belong to them.

Thus, we conclude that *aresenokoitai* is best understood as a reference to men who force themselves sexually on others. This conclusion is consistent with the New Revised Standard Version, the English translation of the Bible often regarded as most scholarly. The New Revised Standard Version translates *arsenokoitai* as "sodomite." As we have already seen, the men of Sodom were the ultimate example of sexual aggression and oppression. Even the New International Version, a more conservative English translation, appears to have been uncomfortable translating *aresenokotai* as a general reference to homosexuality. Instead, in 1 Corinthians 6 they translate the term as "homosexual offender," suggesting that to commit the sin referred to here one must use homosexuality in an aggressive or offensive way.

Finally, there is one more approach for finding the meaning of an obscure word relevant to the present discussion. Etymology is an attempt to trace the origins of a word — not just its component parts or uses after it was created, but where the word originally came from. For a word as old as *arsenokoitai*, doing etymological research is often quite speculative, but some scholars have pointed out that the two Greek words scrunched together to form this new word appear next to each other (as separate words) in Leviticus 20:13 in the *Septuagint*. (The *Septuagint* is the Greek translation of the Old Testament that Paul would have read.) From this, they gather that the word was created by people familiar with this passage, and that Paul was probably referring to the same behavior prohibited by Leviticus 20:13.[29]

This brings us full circle. As we've already seen in our discussion of Old Testament law, Leviticus 20:13 was written in the context of cultic sexual practices, including temple prostitution. In Romans, we saw that Paul was addressing homosexual behavior that occurred in similar cultic situations, where people had abandoned the one true God to worship pagan idols. *If* Paul derived the term *arsenokoitai* from Leviticus 20:13 (and that's a big if), it would follow that Leviticus 20 and Romans 1 would provide the best evidence of the type of homosexual behavior he was intending to prohibit, *i.e.*, cultic sexual practices.

Given the existing state of the literary evidence, it is impossible to know whether Paul was intending to refer to Leviticus 20 or was using the term *arsenokoitai* more broadly to refer to a man who aggressively forces himself on another. For us, it is not necessary to resolve the question. It is sufficient to note that Paul's terminology manifestly does not address the type of behavior we are asking about — two people of the same sex who love each other dearly and live in committed relationship.

In fact, as we have seen, none of the traditional clobber passages addresses this scenario. So, we ask, "Where can we turn for guidance?" The answer is that we must search Scripture for other passages that *do* apply to our question. This is where we'll begin in the next chapter, and we think you'll be surprised to see there are many Scriptures that recognize and affirm the type of homosexual relationships we are talking about. But before jumping into that discussion, let's ask one more question about the clobber passages.

How could so many Christians be wrong?

Searching Christians often ask: "Why have scholars, preachers, and teachers been mistranslating and misunderstanding these passages for so many years?" The answer lies in the fact that people have a natural tendency to care most when their ox is being gored. Let us explain with a story:

A few years back Jeff's spouse, David, was diagnosed with an acoustic neuroma. Probably very few of you know what an acoustic neuroma is, even though you may be able to make an educated guess. For most of you that is all you will ever care to know about acoustic neuromas, but Jeff can tell you specifically that it is a tumor on the acoustic nerve, which runs from the brain stem to the inner ear. He has read a few articles on the subject. But, of course, David knows quite a bit more about the condition than even Jeff does, because when he was diagnosed he spent hours studying everything he could about it.

It's the same with biblical translation and interpretation. For centuries, people have known little about what some of these more obscure biblical words mean. When translators come to a list like the one in 1 Corinthians 6, they might spend some time researching the possible meanings of the words (looking at the roots, looking in more than one dictionary). But unless they have a particular interest at stake, they will probably not study the subject deeply. It wasn't until gay and lesbian theologians and their friends were able to step out of the closet and practice their craft as openly gay and affirming people that some of these more difficult passages were looked into in greater depth. Now, thanks to the scholarship of these people, we have a better understanding of the precise meaning of these passages. *The good news is that none of the clobber passages condemn loving, committed same-sex relationships.* Now let us look at some other Scriptures that *do* apply to our question.

Notes

1   The same word is used in a similar story in Judges 19. However, in that story, a group of men rape a woman to death.

2   Christopher John Farley, *A Beating In Brooklyn,* Time.com: Time Magazine Archive, August 25, 1997.

3   On pages 130 and 147 of *The Construction of Homosexuality* (University of Chicago Press, 1988), David F. Greenberg discusses the use of sexual intercourse as a form of humiliation. Martti Nissinen in *Homoeroticism in the Biblical World* (Fortress Press, Minneapolis, 1998) says, "Homosexual rape has been a traditional way of establishing the relationship with captured enemies and foes." (page 48)

4   Likewise, Jewish scholars did not associate the sin of Sodom and Gomorrah with homosexuality until Philo in the first century AD and

not with any measure of consistency until the sixth century. For a good discussion of this see Greenberg, page 201, footnote 91.

5   Unless otherwise noted, all Scripture quotations are taken from the *New Revised Standard Version.*

6   See Deuteronomy 29:23, 32:32; Isaiah 1:9-17, 3:9, 13:19; Jeremiah 23:14, 49:18, 50:40; Lamentations 4:6; Ezekiel 16:46-56; Amos 4:11; and Zephaniah 2:9.

7   When quoting the clobber passages, we have chosen to use the *King James Version,* because this is the translation most often quoted by Christians who use these passages against gay, lesbian, and bisexual people.

8   For an excellent discussion of this, see Nissinen, pages 91 to 93. In these pages, Nissinen discusses Jewish writings from 200 to 1 BC which associate the sin of the people of Sodom with that of people before the flood of Noah.

9   For example, see JND. Kelly, *A commentary on the Epistles of Peter and of Jude* (Harper and Row, New York, 1969), pages 258-259; Fred Craddock, *First and Second Peter and Jude* (Westminster John Knox Press, Louisville, 1995), page 139; Richard Bauckham, *Jude, 2 Peter* (Word Books, Waco, 1983), page 54; Michael Green, *The Second Epistle General of Peter and the General Epistle of Jude* (Inter-Varsity Press, Leicester, 1987), page 180; CEB. Cranfield, *I and II Peter and Jude* (SCM Press, London, 1960), page 159; and Richard Hays, *The Moral Vision of the New Testament* (Harper, San Francisco, 1996), page 404.

10 For example, see *The Interpreter's Bible Commentary, Vol. X* (Abingdon Press, Nashville, 1987), pages 124-129.

11 Leviticus 18:2-3, 18:24, and 20:23.

12 Some recent scholarship has called this truism into question (*e.g.*, see the article *The end of the male cult prostitute: A literary-historical and sociological analysis of Hebrew qades-qadesim* [Source: *Congress Volume,* pages 37-80, E.J. Brill, Leiden, 1997] by Phyllis A. Bird, published in the *Vetus Testamentum,* 66). But even if these practices were not as prevalent as scholars once thought, the biblical text indicates the biblical authors believed they were, and their writings are based on that factual premise. See also, *Homoeroticism in the Biblical World* by Martti Nissinen, pages 41-42, for a discussion of this.

13   For a lengthy discussion of the worship of Asstarte/Ishtar, see
      Greenberg, pages 95-97.

14   Greenberg, page 92.

15   Nissinen documents how Paul, like other Jewish scholars of his day,
      would have associated homosexual practices with temple prostitution
      (pages 42 and 106). Nissinen also discusses the sex practices of the
      people in Corinth (where Paul is supposed to have written Romans) on
      pages 110 and 113. On pages 95-106 of his book, Greenberg presents a
      thorough discussion of the known examples of male cult prostitution in
      the ancient near east. Pages 158-160 also discuss the unbridled promis-
      cuity of first-century Roman culture.

16   William Arndt, *A Greek-English Lexicon of the New Testament and Other
      Early Christian Literature* (University of Chicago Press, Chicago, 1979),
      page 489.

17   Dale B. Martin, *Arsenokoitês and Malakos: Meaning and Consequences*
      (Source: *Biblical Ethics and Homosexuality: Listening to Scripture* edited
      by Robert L. Brawley; Westminster John Knox Press, Louisville Ken-
      tucky, 1996), page 124. Nissinen also offers "frailty of body or character,
      illness, sentimentality, or moral weakness" as other possibilities for the
      meaning of this word in other contexts (page 117).

18   Martin, page 126.

19   Some have suggested an earlier use of the word in a piece of literature
      called the *Sibylline Oracles*, a collection of oracles written by many
      people over a number of centuries. However, the dating of the particu-
      lar oracle in which this word appears is uncertain. For more on this
      topic see Dale B. Martin's article, page 120.

20   Nissinen, page 114. John Boswell, on page 342 of *Christianity, Social
      Tolerance and Homosexuality*, states that the second half of this word, "is
      a coarse word, generally denoting base or licentious activities (see
      Romans 13:13), and in this and other compounds refers to the vulgar
      English word "f***er".

21   This example, coined by John Boswell in the 1980s, is still the best
      illustration of the troubles inherent in translations based on simple
      root-word analysis.

22   Nissinen, page 115.

23 Martin, pages 120-123. See also John Boswell's *Christianity, Social Tolerance and Homosexuality,* pages 345-348.

24 For a good list of all the instances of *arsenokoitai* and its derivatives in ancient Greek literature, go to http://www.jeramyt.org/gay/arsenok.htm.

25 Arisites, *Apology 13*, Fragmenta 12,9-13.5.4.

26 Hippolytus Scr. Eccl. (Refutation of All Heresies), 060, 5.26.23.4.

27 See notes 17 and 24, above.

28 See Martin's section titled "Arsenokoitês," pages 118-123, for a thorough discussion of contextual clues to the meaning of this word.

29 Robin Scroggs makes this argument on pages 85 and 86 of *The New Testament and Homosexuality* (Fortress Press, Philadelphia, 1983). David Greenberg makes a similar argument on page 214 of *The Construction of Homosexuality.* Although Scroggs, Greenberg, and Nissinen believe the term may refer to some type of homosexual behavior, they do not agree on the type of behavior. For example, Scroggs suggests this may be a reference to male prostitution. Moreover, Nissinen makes the point, on page 117, that our translation of obscure words is always informed by our ideological preconceptions.

Chapter Two

Finding Affirmation in Scripture

In the last chapter we looked at the six biblical passages which are commonly used against gay, lesbian, and bisexual people. And we determined that none of those passages applies to the question we bring to Scripture: Can two people of the same sex, who love God and each other dearly, live in a committed relationship with the blessing of God? Now we will look at passages that *do* address our question.

These stories, which the writers of the Bible included under inspiration of the Holy Spirit, are amazingly gay-positive. However, odds are, you have likely not been taught about these passages and their meaning for sexual minorities. The truth of these texts threatens some of our society's deepest prejudices, and so, unfortunately, their positive messages are usually ignored. It is our hope they will bring comfort and refreshment to the dry areas of your soul.

WARNING: Prejudices can mold our view of the Bible.

At the beginning of *The Adventures of Huckleberry Finn*, young Huck's father is thought to be dead, and a kind woman named Widow Douglas takes him in. Huckleberry tells us there are only a few people he knows who have never lied, and one of them is Widow Douglas. She is portrayed as a kindly Christian who takes care of Huck out of goodness, with no thought of reimbursement. The Widow Douglas tries to "civilize" Huck, teaching him Bible stories and urging him to live a good life and pray often. She is a loving woman who studies her Bible and wants to always do the right thing. She is also a slave owner.

Later in the story, Huck runs away and happens upon Jim, a slave belonging to Widow Douglas's sister, Miss Watson. The sister had intended to sell Jim to a trader in New Orleans. So, fearing he would never see his wife and children again, Jim ran away. He plans to escape to freedom, make some money, and buy his wife and children out of slavery. Huck and Jim's adventures as they travel together down the Mississippi make up the rest of the book.

At every turn, Huck finds himself feeling guilty for "stealing" Miss Watson's "property." He believes he will go to hell for helping Jim escape, and it is clear his Christian education under Widow Douglas is part of the reason he believes this. For all her kindness and goodness, Widow Douglas reads the Bible the same way most of her friends do. She believes slavery is an institution approved by God. She probably believes all African Americans are descended from Ham and the curse recorded in Genesis 9:25-27 demonstrates why they deserve slavery. She sees nothing wrong with buying and selling people because her interpretation of the Bible tells her this is the proper role of those of European descent. In short, she allows her prejudices to mold the way she views the Bible.

This may seem like an extreme example. Only the most bigoted Christian would argue today that the Bible endorses slavery or that Genesis 9:25-27 is a curse against Africans. But Huck's story illustrates how thoroughly we are creatures of our culture and how that culture can create prejudices that get in the way of what God wants to teach us.

This chapter will challenge some of the deepest prejudices of our culture, prejudices that even gay people have often internalized. We will look at Scriptures that dispute some of our most deeply held beliefs, and we must be willing to let God move. In the end, our response will decide if our prejudices mold the Bible, or if we are willing to let the Bible mold us.

The good news at the end of *The Adventures of Huckleberry Finn* is that Miss Watson, who always felt guilty for almost selling Jim to New Orleans, freed him in her will. Perhaps she was able to read the Bible with a fresh perspective. Perhaps she listened to the tugging of God's Spirit on her soul. Whatever the cause, she and Jim were both finally free.

As you read the rest of this chapter, try to set aside any prejudices you may have about the subject. Listen to the Spirit of God speaking through these Scriptures. And perhaps you, like Miss Watson and Jim, will be freed.

Ruth's covenant with Naomi

In the entire Bible, there are only two books named after women. One is Esther, which tells the story of a Jewish woman who becomes Queen of Persia and saves her people from destruction by "coming out" as Jewish to her husband, the king. The other is Ruth, which tells the story of two women who love and support one another through difficult times. Both books contain powerful messages for gay, lesbian, and bisexual people, but it is the story of Ruth that addresses the question we raised in chapter one: Can two people of the same sex live in committed, loving relationship with the blessing of God?

At the beginning of the book of Ruth, we're introduced to Naomi and her husband Elimelech. They are from Bethlehem, where a terrible famine has made it impossible to find food. So, they take their two sons and move to Moab, a foreign land where they believe they'll be able to survive. Unfortunately, Elimelech dies shortly after arriving in Moab. Several years pass, and Naomi's sons marry Ruth and Orpah, two women from the surrounding country. But before they can have children, the sons also die. Naomi, Ruth, and Orpah are left alone with no husbands and no sons.

To understand the full impact of what happened, we need to put ourselves in the mindset of the time. When this story was written, women had only two acceptable places in society: They could be a daughter in their father's household or a wife in their husband's household. A woman without a man had no social standing. There are several stories in the Old Testament about widows who almost starved to death, because they had no man to take care of them.[1] The constant biblical command to "look after widows and orphans" stems from the understanding that widows were among the most vulnerable people in society.

This context makes the next scene almost unbelievable. Naomi, grieving and recognizing her fate as a widow, decides to return to Bethlehem where her father's family is, and where she hopes to find food. She counsels her daughters-in-law to do the same — to return to their own families. She knows she can't offer them any support as a woman, and she fears she'll only be a burden. Orpah, sensibly, returns home. But Ruth clings to Naomi and makes this moving declaration of her intention to stay at Naomi's side, no matter what:

> "Do not press me to leave you or to turn back from following you! Where you go, I will go; where you lodge I will lodge; your people shall be my people, and your God my God. Where you die, I will die — there will I be buried. May the Lord do thus and so to me, and more as well, if even death parts me from you!" (Ruth 1:16-17)

When Ruth spoke those haunting words, "Where you die, I will die — there will I be buried," she wasn't talking about some theoretical distant future. She was giving voice to the very real possibility that her decision to place her life in the hands of another woman could result in death. The sensible thing would have been to allow Naomi to return to her family and for Ruth to return to hers. But Ruth didn't do the sensible thing. She threw caution to the wind and went against every survival instinct. Only one word could explain her actions — love.

After this speech, spoken in the first chapter, the story moves on to tell of Ruth and Naomi's life together. The focus is on the quality of *their* relationship. The biblical storyteller chronicles how Ruth cared for Naomi by taking the only job available to a husbandless woman, gleaning. When the author tells of Ruth's eventual marriage to a much older man, the marriage is portrayed as one of convenience, contrived to help Ruth and Naomi survive the harsh conditions of widowhood. No mention is made of Ruth's love for her husband. And, when Ruth finally bears a son from her marriage, the text focuses on Naomi and her reaction to the great news, not on the father. In fact, the women of the village (and the author) ignore the father entirely, saying, "A son has been born to Naomi." (Ruth 4:17) They remind her that Ruth "who loves you, is more to you than seven sons." (Ruth 4:15) Everyone seems to understand that, for Ruth and Naomi, their most important relationship is the one they share.

Here then is the story the Bible tells: Ruth gave up everything so she could be with Naomi; she put her own life at risk, so she could spend it caring for Naomi; and, even after she married a man, her most important relationship remained the one she shared with Naomi. These actions and emotions are difficult, almost impossible, to explain as mere friendship. If we set aside our preconceptions of what is possible in the Bible, the book of Ruth reads like the story of two women in love.

Instinctively, and perhaps unwittingly, Christians throughout the centuries have acknowledged the validity of this interpretation. The vow Ruth makes to Naomi (quoted above) has been read at Christian weddings for centuries because it so perfectly captures the essence of the love that should exist between spouses. It seems more than a little inconsistent to use these words to define and celebrate spousal love, but then adamantly insist that those who originally spoke the words did not love each other like spouses.

In the first edition of her book *Our Tribe*, Rev. Nancy Wilson, herself a lesbian, tells of a time when she performed in a play that included the story of Ruth and Naomi:

> "After the first or second performance, a young hetero-sexual couple came up to me shyly, saying how much they loved the play, especially the part about Ruth and Naomi — which I had explained in the talk-back with the audience afterward. They liked the passage from Ruth so much that they wanted *my* permission to use it in their wedding ceremony! I was so touched I almost started laughing, but I quite seriously gave them permission, but only if somehow

they could indicate that these words were originally spoken from one woman to another. They cheerfully agreed to my 'terms,' thanked me and left. I [now] have fantasies of interrupting poor, unsuspecting heterosexuals at their wedding with "STOP, in the name of Ruth and Naomi. . . ! Stop stealing our stories while making our relationships illegal or characterizing them as immoral!"[2]

That is precisely what many in the Church have done, roundly condemning any women who dare to share the same vow as Ruth made to Naomi. Yet, how can it be wrong for two women to make these vows when we have the biblical example of Ruth and Naomi doing exactly that?

Some may object, saying, "But the Bible doesn't come right out and say Ruth and Naomi were lovers. It's fine for women to live together and care for each other . . . just nothing else." These people seem to think the main difference between modern lesbian relationships (which they condemn) and the biblical portrayal of Ruth and Naomi (which they accept) is that the Bible doesn't explicitly mention that Ruth and Naomi were sexually intimate. But we challenge that notion. Whether or not Ruth and Naomi were intimate, we believe it is the mere *idea* of two women living in loving, covenantal relationship that many Christians object to.

Imagine a conservative televangelist counseling two women from his congregation. The women say to him, "We want to live together and pledge our love to each other in the sight of God and this congregation. We want our church family to celebrate our relationship. And, for the words of our vows, we want to use Ruth 1:16-17."

He says, "I can't allow that. Our church is against homosexuality."

"Oh," the women say, "that's okay, we'll remain celibate. Think of it as a 'Boston marriage.'"[3]

Do you think the televangelist would say, "Well in that case, let's schedule a date! What about June 5th?" Of course not! The very notion that two women would make such vows to each other is socially repugnant to him. His prejudices tell him this kind of love between members of the same sex is "disgusting." But the Bible is in direct opposition to the televangelist's prejudice.

The Bible is clear. Here we have two women who made vows, lived together for life, loved each other deeply, adopted each other's extended families as their own, and relied on each other for sustenance — as do many lesbian women today. Instead of condemning these relationships, the Bible celebrates them, giving them their own book in Scripture.

However, the book of Ruth is merely the first wave in the Holy Spirit's assault on cultural prejudice against gay people. Other Bible passages pick up where the book of Ruth leaves off. For example, buried within the pages of the Old Testament, in the books of 1 and 2 Samuel, is a story of romantic love between two men, which is neither condemned nor belittled. We will discuss that story next.

What was the nature of Jonathan and David's relationship?

The author of 1 and 2 Samuel is thought to have been a member of King David's court. He seems to know the intimate details of David's life and pulls no punches when telling the story of David's reign, and of his predecessor King Saul. As part of this story, the author tells about Saul's son Jonathan and his unique relationship with David.

You may have heard Jonathan and David's story, but if you're like most people, you have probably never looked at it closely. If your pastor preached about it, the sermon probably talked about the "friendship" of Jonathan and David. Some Christians point to Jonathan and David as an example of idealized male bonding — a type of "brotherly love" not "stained" by the romantic entanglements of male-female relationships. The biblical text, however, is completely inconsistent with this strained interpretation. We will present the biblical evidence and let you be the jury. You decide: Were Jonathan and David merely good friends (experiencing brotherly love), or was there a deeper (romantic) level to their relationship?

The author of 1 Samuel tells of a man named Saul, who became king over Israel and fathered a son named Jonathan. David, who was a shepherd from the smallest of the tribes of Israel, came to the attention of Saul and Jonathan when he volunteered to fight a giant who was troubling their nation. The text tells us David was not afraid because he believed God was on the side of the Israelites. In a show of courage, David fought the giant with only a sling shot and a handful of pebbles. Miraculously, he was victorious. Saul was intrigued by this courageous young man, and so he called David to come talk to him, which brings us to **Exhibit A.** The text says:

> "When David had finished speaking to Saul, the soul of Jonathan was bound to the soul of David, and Jonathan loved him as his own soul. Saul took him that day and would not let him return to his father's house. Then Jonathan made a covenant with David, because he loved him as his own soul. Jonathan stripped himself of the robe that he was wearing, and gave it to David, and his armor, and even his sword and his bow and his belt." (1 Samuel 18:1-4)

Now, imagine if this story had been about Jonathan and a woman. Suppose the author had written that "Jonathan's soul was bound to Mirriam, and Jonathan loved her as his own soul." And suppose that upon meeting Mirriam for the first time, Jonathan immediately gave her all his most precious possessions. (The armor and weapons of a prince were important symbols of his power and status.) If 1 Samuel 18:1-4 were about Jonathan's first encounter with a woman, theologians everywhere would be writing about this as one of the greatest love stories of all time. The story of Jonathan and his love would be the source of dozens of Hollywood films. But because the object of Jonathan's affection is a man, our cultural prejudice kicks in and we insist (notwithstanding the biblical evidence) that this could not have been more than deep friendship.

This "culturally correct" reading will not withstand scrutiny. It asks us to put an interpretation on the story that is completely at odds with our own experience of human behavior. When was the last time you saw a heterosexual man, swept away by brotherly love, offer another man his most precious possessions in their first encounter? Suppose the pastor of your church (assuming he is a man), upon meeting another man for the first time, stripped himself of his suit and gave it to the other. Suppose in that same encounter he also offered his most precious possessions — perhaps a family Bible, a wristwatch with an inscription from his parents, and his beloved four-wheel drive pickup truck. Wouldn't this strike you as more than just a little "queer"? Let's face it, the author of 1 Samuel is describing a classic love-at-first-sight encounter that happens to involve two men.

But there is more to the story than this one meeting. The text goes on to tell us David became a mighty warrior, and his popularity with the people of Israel threatened Saul's throne, so Saul planned to kill David. But Jonathan warned David, and he fled the palace before Saul could act. Eventually, Jonathan convinced his father to allow David back, but Saul soon planned again to kill David. This time he did not tell Jonathan (he'd learned his lesson the first time), but David was able to escape anyway.

Then Jonathan and David met in secret. Jonathan begged David to come back to the palace, but David was afraid for his life. So they made a plan: Jonathan would go home and try to find out what his father was thinking. If his father had cooled down, he would let David know it was safe.

One night, at the royal table, the subject of David came up, and Jonathan spoke on his behalf. Saul's reaction is **Exhibit B.** Saul said to Jonathan:

> "You son of a perverse, rebellious woman! Do I not know that you have chosen [David] the son of Jesse to your own shame and to the shame of your mother's nakedness? For as long as the son of Jesse lives upon the earth, neither you nor your kingdom shall be established." (1 Samuel 20:30)

Many gay men have experienced dinner conversations that sounded very similar to this one. They made the mistake of talking about their lover at the table, and their father became furious. More often than not, the blame goes first to the mother, who was "too soft," or "too harsh," or who "perverted" her son somehow. Then the father turns his anger toward the son: "Can't you see how you're shaming the whole family? Do you even care what this will do to your career? You'll never amount to anything until you give up this foolishness!"

In the biblical text, the arguments are the same. And, even more significantly, Saul's reference to shaming Jonathan's mother's naked-ness carries a sexual connotation. Uncovering the nakedness of a family member was a euphemism for incest in the holiness codes of the Old Testament,[4] and Saul would not have used this phrase lightly. The implication is that Jonathan is bringing sexual shame on his family.

Jonathan immediately ran from the table. And, that night, he went to tell David the sad news. The narrative of their final meeting is full of tragedy and pathos, and constitutes **Exhibit C.**

"David rose from beside the stone heap and prostrated himself with his face to the ground. He bowed three times and they kissed each other and wept with each other; David wept the more. Then Jonathan said to David, 'Go in peace, since both of us have sworn in the name of the Lord, saying, "The Lord shall be between me and you, and between my descendants and your descendants, forever." ' He got up and left; and Jonathan went into the city." (1 Samuel 20:41-42)

This was the last time they would ever see each other. David went into hiding, and Jonathan was eventually killed in battle, alongside his father. Perhaps they had some idea this was the end. They certainly knew their love was doomed. And Jonathan reminded David of their covenant with each other. He reminded him that even if they could not be together, they had made a pledge and the bond between them would last through all generations. All their children and grandchildren would be like one family, bound by their love for each other. Later, after taking the throne, David would remember this covenant and adopt Jonathan's only son as his own — something completely unheard of in a time when kings were expected to kill anyone with any connection to a previous, rival king.[5]

So, we ask, was this merely deep friendship or a romantic relationship? In Exhibit A, upon their first meeting, Jonathan is said to have loved David as his own soul and to have given him his most precious possessions. In Exhibit B, Jonathan's father uses language of sex and shame when he decries Jonathan and David's relationship in a fit of rage. In Exhibit C, we see Jonathan and David's passionate, tearful goodbye, and Jonathan reminding David of the eternal covenant they have made to each other — a covenant David still honors years later, even though honoring it is politically incorrect. But if you are still not convinced this was a romantic relationship, there is one more piece of biblical evidence — the smoking gun, so to speak. The story has one more passionate chapter.

In the first chapter of 2 Samuel, the author tells us that after Saul and Jonathan were killed in battle, David tore his clothes and fasted, a sign of deep mourning. He wept and wrote a song, which he ordered all the people of Judah to sing. In that song, he included these words, which are **Exhibit D:**

"Saul and Jonathan, beloved and lovely!
In life and in death they were not divided;
they were swifter than eagles,
they were stronger than lions.

How the mighty have fallen in the midst of battle!
Jonathan lies slain upon your high places.
I am distressed for you my brother Jonathan;

Greatly beloved were you to me;
your love to me was wonderful, passing the love of women."
(2 Samuel 1:23, 26-27, emphasis added)

Here it is in black and white. David states the love he shared with Jonathan was greater than what he had experienced with women. Have you ever heard a heterosexual man say he loved his male friend more than his wife? This goes well beyond deep friendship between two heterosexual men.

In this story, we have a direct biblical answer to our question: Can two people of the same sex live in a loving, committed relationship with God's favor? The answer is "yes," because Jonathan and David did, and the Bible celebrates their relationship.

The author feels no need to explain away the love between these two men, putting in a note saying "this may look like a love story, but no hanky-panky happened." When King Saul assumes the relationship is much more than friendship, the author leaves Saul's comments in, and lets the reader assume the same. The author also would have been aware of this story's similarity to other ancient Near-eastern stories that contained homoerotic aspects.[6] He would have known his story would be interpreted by readers of his time with these other accounts in mind, yet he did not bother to differentiate Jonathan and David's relationship.

Under inspiration of the Holy Spirit, the author of 1 and 2 Samuel wrote this beautiful love story and saw no conflict between it and the earlier Scriptures in Leviticus. How is this possible? Apparently the author of 1 and 2 Samuel understood the Leviticus passage the same way we do, seeing it as a condemnation of Canaanite temple sex which, therefore, had no application to a deep romantic relationship between two men who loved and served the God of Israel. If someone had challenged the author of 1 and 2 Samuel, he might well have responded, "This is not what Leviticus was meant to condemn. You've got to understand the context in which Leviticus was written. This is a very different situation."

Why can't we use the same common sense today? Why are some Christians so determined to condemn what God has so clearly approved in Scripture?

Remember, David is not some minor hero in the Bible. He is

called "a man after God's own heart." (1 Samuel 13:14) He is one of Israel's best-loved kings. He is one of the most prolific writers of Scripture (writing many of the Psalms). He is in the lineage of Jesus Christ. And he loved Jonathan.[7]

The Ethiopian eunuch: Despised and rejected, but not by God

This story challenges what Jeff calls the "grasshopper mentality," a phrase he gets from an old joke about a grasshopper in a bar. (If you come from a conservative background like we do, to understand the joke, you need to know there's a mixed drink called a "grasshopper.")

A grasshopper steps up to a bar and says, "I'd like a drink, please."
The bartender asks, "What'll it be?"
"I don't know. What do you suggest?"
"Well," the bartender says, "you may not know it, but we have a drink named after *you!*"
At this, the grasshopper grins and says, "In that case, I'll have a *Stuart!*"

You see, the bartender had been unable to see past the grasshopper's "type" to think he might have a name, a family, and a life beyond his "grasshopperness." And that is the way many Christians view gay, lesbian, and bisexual people. Once they find out someone is gay, it is as if that person has a neon sign on his or her forehead, flashing, "GAY! GAY! GAY!" But God sees people differently, looking past incidental labels and seeing into the core of each being. As the Apostle Peter says, "God shows no partiality." (Acts 10:34) The grace of God is available to gay people on the same basis as all other humans. That is what the story of Philip and the Ethiopian eunuch is all about.

The author of Acts sought to write a well-researched history of the acts of the apostles following the resurrection of Jesus and his ascension into heaven. In chapter eight of that book, we find Philip heading a great evangelistic campaign in Samaria. The story tells us that along with "proclaiming the Messiah," (8:4) Philip was healing people and casting out demons. His efforts were going so well, and so many were coming to faith, "there was great joy in that city." (8:8) However, in the midst of this great revival, the Holy Spirit told Philip to "get up and go toward the south to the road that goes down from Jerusalem to Gaza." (8:26) This road was in the wilderness.

This seems like a strange command: Leave the great revival among the Samaritans, and go out into the wilderness. But Philip did what God asked. Then the story gets even stranger. Out in the wilderness, Philip finds a lone Ethiopian eunuch traveling south from Jerusalem. The author tells us the man was sitting in his chariot, reading from Isaiah. Having just been to Jerusalem to worship, he was now headed home.

It is this nameless man who makes the story so important to gay, lesbian, and bisexual Christians. So, let us look more closely at the identity of the Ethiopian eunuch. At the time of the writing of Acts, the term Ethiopian was used to describe people from Nubia, south of Egypt. So, we know from this description that he was probably a black African. But that still leaves us with the question, "What is a eunuch?"

The Greek word used in Acts is *eunouchos*, which means literally "guardian or keeper of the couch."[8] The term refers to those who were placed in positions of highest trust in royal palaces and wealthy households. Eunuchs served and guarded the women in these households. Because of their intimate access to the royal courts, eunuchs often rose to senior government positions. In this story, the Ethiopian eunuch was Treasurer to the Queen of Ethiopia. (8:27)

Not just anyone was permitted to serve as a eunuch. Given their intimate access to the women of the household, they had to be men who could be trusted not to have affairs with (or force themselves upon) the women — because to do so would cloud the line of succession to the throne and confuse inheritance rights. It doesn't take a rocket scientist to figure out that the ideal candidate for the position of eunuch would be someone known for his disinterest in women. Although the ancients did not have the same clear concept of heterosexual and homosexual that we do today, people were put together in the same way then as now. There were men then (as now) who had a reputation for being disinterested in women as objects of sexual attraction. They would make the ideal eunuch.

Of course, it was not always possible to find someone like this. In those situations, or in situations where the master wanted to be extra cautious, eunuchs were often castrated, *i.e.*, their testicles were removed so they would be incapable of fathering children. But it would be historically inaccurate to picture eunuchs as a bunch of straight men who were castrated. Ancient literature indicates that various types of eunuchs were recognized. There were "manmade eunuchs," meaning those who had been castrated. But there are also references to so-called "natural" or "born" eunuchs. This category apparently included males who from childhood seemed incapable of or disinterested in intercourse with women.[9]

For example, in the Jewish Babylonian Talmud, which was written several hundred years after Christ but is based on an oral tradition that goes back much further, Rabbi Eliezer refers to "eunuchs by nature" and contrasts them with manmade eunuchs. He asserts that natural eunuchs can be "cured," a statement that would make no sense if he were talking about men who had physical genital defects.[10]

In the same Talmud, other rabbis discuss how a natural eunuch can be identified. Signs of natural eunuchs are said to include lateness of pubic hair, urine that does not form an arch, absence of a beard, softness of hair, smoothness of skin, a high voice, and a body that does not steam when bathing in winter.[11] Are you starting to get the picture? The ancient stereotype of "natural" or "born" eunuchs sounds hauntingly like the modern stereotype of gay men as effeminate sissy-boys who need to be "cured" because something is wrong with them.

And what was "wrong" with them? It is clear from the ancient literature that eunuchs as a class had a reputation for being attracted sexually to men, rather than women. For example, an ancient Summarian myth about the creation of eunuchs says they "do not satisfy the lap of women." They were specifically created, the myth says, because they can resist the wiles of women.[12] The book of Sirach, found in the Old Testament of the Catholic Bible, says that embracing a girl makes a eunuch groan. (Sirach 30:20)

The Roman playwright Juvenal (who lived near the time of Christ) stated, "When a soft eunuch takes to matrimony... it is hard *not* to write a satire."[13] Lucian, a Greek satirist who lived about one hundred years after Christ, compares a eunuch with a concubine to a deaf man with a flute, a bald man with a comb, and a blind man with a mirror.[14] In other words, a eunuch has as much need for a woman as a fish has for a bicycle.

Instead, eunuchs were commonly associated in ancient culture with sexual interest in men. For example, the *Kama Sutra* (an ancient Eastern sacred text) has an entire chapter on eunuchs seducing men.[15] Quintus Curtius, an historian who wrote about Alexander the Great, reports that Alexander's palace included "herds of eunuchs, also accustomed to prostitute themselves [like women]."[16] Quintus Curtius also reports that Alexander the Great fell deeply in love with a eunuch named Bagoas and they entered into a relationship of mutual love.

These examples from ancient literature indicate that, in ancient culture, eunuchs were a suspect category. They were commonly regarded as being sexually interested in men, not women. This does not mean all were gay. But clearly, as a class, they were strongly associated with homosexual desire in the popular mind. To introduce one's self as a eunuch in ancient times was roughly akin to introducing one's self today as a hairdresser from San Francisco.

With this historical background, we can now return to the story in Acts 8 about the Ethiopian eunuch. The point we have been leading up to is this: When the Ethiopian introduced himself to Philip as a eunuch, Philip would have immediately known he was dealing with a man who was part of a class commonly associated with homosexual desire.

Acts 8:32-33 tells us the Ethiopian eunuch was reading from Isaiah 53:7-8. This passage was seen by early Christians as a prophecy about Jesus. The whole chapter tells about the suffering of God's anointed one. Verse 3 says, "He was despised and rejected by others." Verse 7 says, "He was oppressed and he was afflicted." It seems like a strange passage for someone to read just after worshipping in Jerusalem, the holy city. But it makes sense when we understand that the Ethiopian eunuch had probably found *himself* despised and rejected by the religious leaders in Jerusalem.

Just like gay, lesbian, and bisexual people of today, eunuchs were the sexual outcasts of Jewish religious society. Deuteronomy 23:1 states, "No one whose testicles are crushed or whose penis is cut off shall be admitted to the assembly of the LORD." By the first century, this verse was understood as applying to anyone who was incapable of fathering children (either physically or by reason of what we today would call sexual orientation). The first-century teachers of Jewish law forbade converting such a person to Judaism, and they would have informed the Ethiopian eunuch when he arrived in Jerusalem that he could not even enter the outer court of the temple. Tom Horner tells us, "The eunuch was *persona non grata* both socially and religiously."[17]

So, in Jerusalem, the Ethiopian eunuch would have been assured by the people of God that he could not become one of them. He would have been despised and rejected, cut off from God's grace by the religious leaders.

Perhaps someone among his friends had furtively told him about Isaiah 56:3-5, which promises eunuchs who keep God's commandments that someday they will receive a house, a monument, and a name within God's walls. Perhaps, like gay, lesbian, and bisexual Christians today, he had gone to his religious leaders pointing to the Scriptures which affirmed him, hoping he might somehow be accepted. But instead, he had been clobbered once again with Deuteronomy 23:1. A eunuch "may not enter the assembly of God's people!" And so he had taken his precious scroll of Isaiah and begun his journey home, reading about another of God's children who had been despised, rejected, and cut off.

It was at this point Philip, guided by the Holy Spirit, happened

along and asked, "Do you understand what you are reading?" The
Ethiopian eunuch, still seeking a religious authority figure, answered
"How can I unless someone guides me?" (8:31) So, Philip started
with this Scripture and "proclaimed to him the good news of Jesus."
(8:35) Then they came to some water and the eunuch said, "Look,
here is some water! What is to prevent me from being baptized?"
Philip's answer should be astonishing to anyone who still holds a
prejudice against gay, lesbian, and bisexual believers.

Philip responded, "If you believe with all your heart, you may."
Philip did not say, "Let's talk about Deuteronomy 23:1." He also
did not say, "I realize since you're a eunuch that you may desire men;
can you promise me you'll never have a sexual relationship with a
man?" Instead, operating under the inspiration of the Holy Spirit,
Philip said, "If you believe with all your heart, you may." We have no
way of knowing whether the Ethiopian eunuch was in fact gay. But
we do know he was part of a class of people commonly associated
with homosexuality and that this fact was completely irrelevant to
whether he could become a Christian.

The implications of this story are profound for gay, lesbian, and
bisexual people. This story illustrates that what matters is how we
relate to Jesus — a point made over and over again in the New
Testament, but which many modern Christians refuse to apply
consistently. Scripture is not what keeps them from accepting their
gay and lesbian brothers and sisters; only prejudice does. For if there
were some authentic scriptural basis for excluding the Ethiopian
eunuch because of the real possibility he was homosexual, we can be
sure that Philip, a man who followed God even when God led him
into the wilderness, would have been quick to pursue it.

But there are still two more key Scriptures to examine, both
found in the Gospels.

Diversity in creation

Some Christians confidently assert that God did not create
homosexual people "that way." This is important because they realize

if God did create gays "that way," rejecting them would be tantamount to rejecting God's work in creation. In pressing their "creation order" argument, some Christians are fond of saying, "God made Adam and Eve, not Adam and Steve!" To bolster their position, they often cite Jesus' words in Matthew 19:4-5, where he responds to a question about whether divorce is permissible:

> "Jesus answered, 'Have you not read that the One who made them at the beginning made them male and female, and said, "For this reason a man shall leave his father and mother and be joined to his wife and the two shall become one flesh"? Therefore, what God has joined together, let no one separate.' "

From these words, some Christians draw the conclusion that heterosexuality is the creation norm and, thus, heterosexual marriage is the only legitimate way for people to form romantic relationships. Ironically, Jesus' own words *in this very same passage* refute these conclusions.

As the dialogue continues, Jesus' disciples are disturbed by his strict teaching on divorce. The disciples say that if divorce is not a ready option, perhaps it would be best for a man not to marry a woman. Jesus responds:

> "Not everyone can accept this teaching, but only those to whom it is given. For there are eunuchs who have been so from birth, and there are eunuchs who have been made eunuchs by others, and there are eunuchs who have made themselves eunuchs for the sake of the kingdom of heaven. Let anyone accept this who can." (Matthew 19:11-12)

Here Jesus identifies three classes of men who should not marry women. Taking his categories in reverse order, first, there are those who have made themselves "eunuchs" for the kingdom of heaven, *i.e.,* those who foreswear marriage to better serve God. Second, he mentions those who have been "made eunuchs by others," an apparent reference to castrated males. But Jesus mentions a third category — eunuchs who were born that way. Some might argue that Jesus was referring to males born without testicles, but this would be extremely rare. Moreover, this interpretation ignores how the term "born eunuchs" was used in other literature of the time.

As we have already seen, in the ancient world, including ancient Jewish culture (as reflected in the Talmud), "natural" or "born" eunuchs were not associated with missing testicles. Rather, they were associated with stereotypically effeminate characteristics and behavior (just like modern gay men), and were thought by Rabbi Eliezer to be subject to "cure" (just like modern gays). Moreover, as we have also seen, eunuchs were commonly associated with homosexual desire. As a reasonably informed person of his time, Jesus would have been aware of this common view of eunuchs. Yet he very matter-of-factly asserts that some people are simply born that way. The implication of his statement is profound — God created gay people the way they are! Jesus says so.

Unlike Rabbi Eliezer, Jesus feels no need to "cure" these born eunuchs. He speaks no words of condemnation. Rather he lists people born gay alongside another honored class (eunuchs for the kingdom), and accepts them as a natural part of God's creation order.

Thus, when Matthew 19 is read as a whole, we see Jesus teaches that *most* people are created for heterosexual marriage. (We too accept this as God's predominant creation paradigm.) But, unlike some modern Christians, Jesus does not see this as the only honorable way to live. He acknowledges that some human beings have been created by God to follow a less common, but equally legitimate path. There are some who have been eunuchs from birth — made that way by God.

But we're not quite done. In fact, we've saved the best for last.

When Jesus met a gay person

From our days in Sunday school, many of us are familiar with the Gospel story where Jesus healed the servant of a Roman centurion.

This story is recorded in Matthew 8:5-13 and Luke 7:1-10. In Matthew, we are told that the centurion came to Jesus to plead for the healing of his servant. Jesus said he was willing to come to the centurion's house, but the centurion said there was no need for Jesus to do so — he believed that if Jesus simply spoke the word, his servant would be healed. Marveling at the man's faith, Jesus pronounced the servant healed. Luke tells a similar story.

Just another miracle story, right? Not on your life!

In the original language, the importance of this story for gay, lesbian, and bisexual Christians is much clearer. The Greek word used in Matthew's account to refer to the servant of the centurion is *pais*. In the language of the time, *pais* had three possible meanings depending upon the context in which it was used. It could mean "son or boy;" it could mean "servant," or it could mean a particular type of servant — one who was "his master's male lover."[18] Often these lovers were younger than their masters, even teenagers.

To our modern minds, the idea of buying a teen lover seems repugnant. But we have to place this in the context of ancient cultural norms. In ancient times, commercial transactions were the predominant means of forming relationships. Under the law, the wife was viewed as the property of the husband, with a status just above that of slave. Moreover, in Jesus' day, a boy or girl was considered of marriageable age upon reaching his or her early teens. It was not uncommon for boys and girls to marry at age 14 or 15.[19] Nor was it uncommon for an older man to marry a young girl. Fortunately civilization has advanced, but these were the norms in the culture of Jesus' day.

In that culture, if you were a gay man who wanted a male "spouse," you achieved this, like your heterosexual counterparts, through a commercial transaction — purchasing someone to serve that purpose. A servant purchased to serve this purpose was often called a *pais*.

The word *boy* in English offers a rough comparison. Like *pais*, the word *boy* can be used to refer to a male child. But in the slave South in the nineteenth century, *boy* was also often used to refer to male slaves. The term *boy* can also be used as a term of endearment. For example, Jeff's father often refers to his mother as "his girl." He doesn't mean that she is a child, but rather that she is his "special one." The term *boy* can be used in the same way, as in "my boy" or "my beau." In ancient Greek, *pais* had a similar range of meanings.

Thus, when this term was used, the listener had to consider the context of the statement to determine which meaning was intended. Some modern Christians may be tempted to simply declare by fiat that the Gospels could not possibly have used the term *pais* in the sense of male lover, end of discussion. But that would be yielding to prejudice. We must let the word of God speak for itself, even if it leads us to an uncomfortable destination.

Is it possible the *pais* referred to in Matthew 8 and Luke 7 was the Roman centurion's male lover? Let's look at the biblical evidence.

The Bible provides three key pieces of textual and circumstantial evidence. First, in the Luke passage, several additional Greek words are used to describe the one who is sick. Luke says this *pais* was the centurion's *entimos duolos*. The word *duolos* is a generic term for slave, and was never used in ancient Greek to describe a son/boy. Thus, Luke's account rules out the possibility the sick person was the centurion's son; his use of *duolos* makes clear this was a slave. However, Luke also takes care to indicate this was no ordinary slave. The word *entimos* means "honored." This was an "honored slave" (*entimos duolos)* who was his master's *pais.* Taken together, the three Greek words preclude the possibility the sick person was either the centurion's son or an ordinary slave, leaving only one viable option — he was his master's male lover.[20]

A second piece of evidence is found in verse 9 of Matthew's account. In the course of expressing his faith in Jesus' power to heal by simply speaking, the centurion says, "When I tell my slave to do something, he does it." By extension, the centurion concludes that Jesus is also able to issue a remote verbal command that must be carried out. When speaking here of his slaves, the centurion uses the word *duolos.* But when speaking of the one he is asking Jesus to heal, he uses only *pais*. In other words, when he is quoted in Matthew, the centurion uses *pais* only when referring to the sick person. He uses a different word, *duolos*, when speaking of his other slaves, as if to draw a distinction. (In Luke, it is others, not the centurion, who call the sick one an *entimos duolos*.) Again, the clear implication is that the sick man was no ordinary slave. And when *pais* was used to describe a servant who was not an ordinary slave, it meant only one thing — a slave who was the master's male lover.

The third piece of evidence is circumstantial. In the Gospels, we have many examples of people seeking healing for themselves or for family members. But this story is the only example of someone seeking healing for a slave. The actions described are made even more remarkable by the fact that this was a proud Roman centurion (the conqueror/oppressor) who was humbling himself and pleading with a Jewish rabbi (the conquered/oppressed) to heal his slave. The extraordinary lengths to which this man went to seek healing for his slave is much more understandable, from a psychological perspective, if the slave was his beloved companion.

Thus, all the textual and circumstantial evidence in the Gospels points in one direction. For objective observers, the conclusion is inescapable: In this story Jesus healed a man's male lover. When understood this way, the story takes on a whole new dimension.

Imagine how it may have happened. While stationed in Palestine, the centurion's *pais* becomes ill — experiencing some type of life-threatening paralysis. The centurion will stop at nothing to save him. Perhaps a friend tells him of rumors of Jesus' healing powers. Perhaps this friend also tells him Jesus is unusually open to foreigners, teaching his followers that they should love their enemies, even Roman soldiers. So the centurion decides to take a chance. Jesus was his only hope.

As he made his way to Jesus, he probably worried about the possibility that Jesus, like other Jewish rabbis, would take a dim view of his homosexual relationship. Perhaps he even considered lying. He could simply use the word *duolos*. That would have been accurate, as far as it went. But the centurion probably figured if Jesus was powerful enough to heal his lover, he was also powerful enough to see through any half-truths.

So the centurion approaches Jesus and bows before him. "Rabbi, my . . . ," the word gets caught in his throat. This is it — the moment of truth. Either Jesus will turn away in disgust, or something wonderful will happen. So, the centurion clears his throat and speaks again. "Rabbi, my *pais* — yes, my *pais* lies at home sick unto death." Then he pauses and waits for a second that must have seemed like an eternity. The crowd of good, God-fearing people surrounding Jesus probably became tense. This was like a gay man asking a televangelist to heal his lover. What would Jesus do?

Without hesitation, Jesus says, "Then I will come and heal him."

It's that simple! Jesus didn't say, "Are you kidding? I'm not going to heal your *pais* so you can go on living in sin!" Nor did he say, "Well, it shouldn't surprise you that your *pais* is sick; this is God's judgment on your relationship."

Instead, Jesus' words are simple, clear, and liberating for all who have worried about what God thinks of gay relationships. "I will come and heal him."

At this point, the centurion says there is no need for Jesus to travel to his home. He has faith that Jesus' word is sufficient. Jesus then turns to the good people standing around him — those who were already dumbfounded that he was willing to heal this man's male lover. To them, Jesus says in verse 10 of Matthew's account, "I have not found faith this great anywhere in Israel." In other words, Jesus holds up this gay centurion as an example of the type of faith others should aspire to.

Jesus didn't just tolerate this gay centurion. He said he was an example of faith — someone we all should strive to be like.

Then, just so the good, God-fearing people wouldn't miss his point, Jesus speaks again in verse 11: "I tell you, many will come from the east and the west [*i.e.,* beyond the borders of Israel] to find a seat in the kingdom of heaven, while the heirs [*i.e.,* those considered likely to inherit heaven] will be thrown into outer darkness." By this statement Jesus affirmed that many others like this gay centurion — those who come from beyond the assumed boundaries of God's grace — are going to be admitted to the kingdom of heaven. And he also warned that many who think themselves the most likely to be admitted will be left out.

With this story, we rest our case. Who could ask for more? In this story, Jesus restores a gay relationship by a miracle of healing and then holds up a gay man as an example of faith for all to follow. What more do our fundamentalist friends want? Who is Lord — Jesus or cultural prejudice?

Majority rules?

Once upon a time, there were four Jewish rabbis who engaged in lively theological debates. One of them was always the odd man out. The other three would gang up on him, criticizing his positions. One day, after the usual "three-to-one, majority-rules" conclusion to a discussion, the fourth rabbi decided to appeal to a higher authority.

"Dear God," he cried, "I know I am right. Please give a sign to prove it to my colleagues."

Suddenly a dark storm cloud arose in the midst of a blue sky, moved directly over the four rabbis, rumbled, and dissolved.

"See, I'm right!" the fourth rabbi shouted. The other three disagreed, pointing out that storm clouds often form on hot summer days.

"Dear God," the rabbi prayed, "I need a better sign."

This time four storm clouds appeared, joined as one, and a lightning bolt struck a tree near the rabbis.

"I told you I was right!" the fourth rabbi exclaimed. But his friends insisted nothing had happened that could not be explained by natural causes.

Just as the fourth rabbi was getting ready to ask for a really big sign, the sky turned black, the earth shook, and a powerful voice from the sky bellowed, "HE'S RIGHT!"

"Well?" the fourth rabbi said.

"So?" one of the others said. "Now it's 3 to 2."

As the joke points out, it's not easy to change people's minds. Sometimes one wonders if even God's voice thundering from heaven would be enough to cause some of our Christian friends to accept those who are gay, lesbian, or bisexual. Fortunately, truth is not determined by majority vote.

If it were, Christians would still own slaves, women and blacks would still have no vote, Jews, Muslims, and suspected witches would still be summarily executed, and gay people would have little reason for hope. But as Dr. Martin Luther King, Jr., once said, "Truth pressed to the ground will rise again!" The truth of the Scriptures examined in the foregoing pages will eventually prevail over prejudice.

For the Bible could not be clearer. Everywhere the Bible confronts loving, committed homosexual relationships, they are affirmed. By contrast, the passages commonly used against gay people are all set firmly in the context of promiscuous, idolatrous sexual behavior. When these passages addressing promiscuous behavior are ripped out of context and used as blanket condemnations of loving, committed homosexual relationships, the Scriptures are placed in hopeless conflict. The careful, contextual approach we have suggested is the only one that can harmonize all the Scriptures that address homosexuality.

The good news is the Bible teaches that *anyone* who believes in Jesus Christ will be accepted into God's realm. You can be a child of God and live in loving, committed relationship with another person of the same sex. We stake our claim on the stories of Ruth and Naomi, and Jonathan and David, on the response of Philip to the Ethiopian eunuch, and on the words and teachings of Jesus Christ himself.

Notes

1   For examples, see the stories of widows who came to Elijah and Elisha for help (1 Kings 17:10-24 and 2 Kings 4:1-37), and the story of the woman from Tekoa who confronted David (2 Samuel 14:4-12). Also, in Genesis 38, Judah tells his daughter-in-law Tamar to return to her father's house, because her husband has died, illustrating the two possibilities available to a woman.

2   Rev. Nancy Wilson, *Our Tribe: Queer Folks, God, Jesus and the Bible* (HarperSanFrancisco, 1995), page 157.

3   In *Our Tribe*, Nancy Wilson states, " 'Boston marriage' is a term from the Victorian era, used for women who lived together in lifelong committed friendships that were, it was assumed, devoid of sex." (page 291.) The video *Out of the Past* (Unapix Entertainment, Inc., New York, 1998) documents how these marriages were accepted in the upper classes of most East coast cities (like Boston), until the women's suffrage movement made them too threatening to the male political structure.

4   Leviticus 18:6-18 begins, "You shall not approach anyone near of kin to uncover nakedness" and goes on to list every possible incestuous relationship (except that of father and daughter), stating before each one, "You shall not uncover the nakedness of . . ."

5   The story of David adopting Jonathan's son Mephibosheth is found in 2 Samuel 9. For examples of how some other monarchs dealt with the potential heirs to the throne, see 2 Kings 10:1-11 and 11:1-3, 13-16.

6   On pages 20-24 of *Homoeroticism in the Biblical World*, Martti Nissinen does a good job discussing the *Epic of Gilgamesh*, which he says is "sometimes considered the most important ancient Near Eastern depiction of homoeroticism." (Page 20.) In this story, Gilgamesh is described as a half-man half-god, whose energy for sex and adventure are endless. He ravages the young men and women of Uruk so uncontrollably that the people of Uruk call to the creator goddess to create him a suitable partner, so he will leave them alone. The creator goddess makes a red-haired man named Enkidu, and the adventures of Gilgamesh and Enkidu make up the rest of the tale. David F. Greenberg also discusses the *Epic of Gilgamesh*, along with other examples of Near Eastern homosexual warrior love relationships on pages 110-116 of *The Construction of Homosexuality*. He states, "Parallels to the Gilgamesh-Enkidu relationship have often been seen in the biblical stories of David and Jonathan, and in the devotion of Achilles and Patrocles for one another in the *Illiad*." (Page 113) For further discussion of the Epic of Gilgamesh and how it might have been used by the writers of the Bible, see also *Reading the Old Testament* (Wadsworth Publishing Company, Belmont, CA, 1999) by Barry L. Bandstra, pages 76-77.

7   The Bible tells us both David and Jonathan married. (1 Samuel 25:39-42; 2 Samuel 3:14; 4:4; 9:3-7; 11:27) This is not inconsistent with a

romantic relationship between them. Even today, many homosexual people marry and bear children to conform to social pressures. As a prince, Jonathan would have had no choice but to marry, so as to bear a son to become his heir. David would have faced similar pressures. Other Bible stories indicate David was capable of feeling lust for women. (2 Samuel 11:2-26) He appears to have been what we today would call a bisexual — someone capable of forming a deep romantic relationship with persons of either sex. By contrast, based on what we find in Scripture, David seems to have been Jonathan's only sincere romantic interest. He appears to have been what we today would call a gay man.

8   *The Keeper of the Bed: The Story of the Eunuch* (Arlington Books, London, 1973) by Charles Humana, page 21. *Note:* Our discussion in the next few pages is drawn from the work of several authors, including Rev. Nancy Wilson in *Our Tribe*, Michael S. Piazza in *Holy Homosexuals: The Truth About Being Gay or Lesbian and Christian, Second Edition* (Sources of Hope Publishing House, Dallas, Texas, 1995), David F. Greenberg in *The Construction of Homosexuality,* and Faris Malik in *Born Eunuchs: Homosexual Identity in Ancient World* (http://www.well.com/user/aquarius/thesis.htm).

9   Faris Malik, Introduction to *Born Eunuchs.*

10 *Talmud Bavli, Tractate Yevumos* (The Schottenstein Edition, Mesorah Publications Ltd., Brooklyn, NY, 1999), Chapter 8, 79b.

11 *Talmud Bavli, Tractate Yevumos,* Chapter 8, 80b.

12 *Inanna's Descent into the Nether World,* (*Journal of Cuneiform Studies,* Vol. 4, # 4, 1950), page 200.

13 *Juvenal and Persius* (Harvard University Press, Cambridge, MA, 1957), translated by G. G. Ramsay, page 5, emphasis added.

14 *Lucian, Volume III* (William Heinemann, London, 1921), translated by A.M. Harmon, page 197.

15 *Kama Sutra* (Castle Books, New York, 1963), Part II, Chapter 9.

16 Quintus Curtius, *History of Alexander, Volume II* (Harvard University Press, Cambridge, 1956), translated by John C. Rolfe, page 51.

17 Tom Horner, *Jonathan Loved David* (Westminster Press, Philadelphia, 1978), page 124. In *Homoeroticism in the Biblical World,* Martti Nissinen

states that "any eunuch attempting to join the Christian community would have had to deliberately ignore the Torah (Old Testament Jewish Scriptures), which forbade it." Robin Scroggs, in *The New Testament and Homosexuality,* details how Philo, a first century Jewish philosopher, not only upheld the ban on eunuchs, but associated eunuchs with Roman male homosexual prostitutes.

18   K.J. Dover, *Greek Homosexuality* (Harvard University Press, Cambridge, 1978), page 16; Bernard Sergent, *Homosexuality in Greek Myth* (Beacon Press, Boston, 1986), page 10.

19   *Mercer Dictionary of the Bible* (Mercer University Press, Macon, 1994), page 554.

20   For an excellent and thorough discussion of the terms *pais* and *entimos duolos* in these two gospel accounts, see Donald Mader's article *The Entimos Pais of Matthew 8:5-13 and Luke 7:1-10,* (Source: *Homosexuality and Religion and Philosophy,* Harland Publishing, Inc., New York, 1998).

Chapter Three

How Jesus Applied Scripture

We believe the evidence presented in the first two chapters is conclusive. But suppose someone doesn't yet share our confidence. (Letting go of years of negative teaching isn't easy.) Suppose, for example, Romans 1 really was meant to condemn even loving, committed same-sex relationships. Would that be the end of the discussion?

Many would say yes, because they've been taught an approach to spiritual decision-making that is summed up in the bumper-sticker phrase: "The Bible says it. I believe it. That settles it!"

In point of fact, however, there is no one — not one person on the face of the earth (at least that we've ever met) — who lives consistently by that bumper sticker. No Christian, even the most fundamentalist, keeps every rule found in the Bible.

More than 613 rules, but which ones apply?

Jewish scholars, attempting to make it possible for observant Jews to follow God's law exactly, have catalogued 613 commandments in the first five books of the Bible.[1] Many of these rules have to do with animal sacrifices in the temple. Many more include instructions on which foods are appropriate to eat, what types of clothing one should wear, what to do if a person has a skin disease, and other details of everyday life. Some of the rules (such as the Ten Commandments) are well-known, even to non-religious people. Others are so obscure only biblical scholars can trace their intricacies. It's important to note that the vast majority of these rules are not observed by Christians today. There are also some rather prominent New Testament rules that Christians — even the most conservative — no longer follow.

To test our proposition, think of the most conservative Christian you know and check off the rules in the following list that she or he applies consistently:

☐ *"You shall not round off the hair on your temples, or mar the edges of your beard." Leviticus 19:27*
Of course, any man who shaves his beard breaks this rule. However, to apply it consistently a man cannot even trim the edges of his beard. So, any Christian man who doesn't look like Billy Gibbons from ZZ Top is violating this rule.

☐ *"Women should be silent in the churches. For they are not permitted to speak, but should be subordinate as the law also says. If there is anything they desire to know, let them ask their husbands at home."*
1 Corinthians 14:34-35
Think of the most conservative Christian woman you know. Does she ever speak in church? Even if she whispers a question in someone's ear, instead of waiting to ask her husband at home, she is violating this rule. Conservative churches that don't allow women to preach, but allow them to testify at prayer meetings or teach Sunday school classes are also violating this New Testament rule.

☐ *"But any woman who prays or prophesies with her head unveiled disgraces her head — it is one and the same thing as having her head shaved." 1 Corinthians 11:5*
Some Catholic churches, particularly in Latin American countries, still require women to wear head coverings in the sanctuary, and there are some conservative Christian groups which require women to wear head coverings at all times (so they'll always be ready, if they need to pray). So, it might be possible the person you're thinking of applies this rule, at least fairly consistently. But, as noted in Chapter 1, the vast majority of even fundamentalist Christians ignore this New Testament rule.

☐ *"You shall not put on a garment made of two materials."*
Leviticus 19:19

Anyone who wears a cotton-polyester blend, or who owns a seersucker suit violates this rule. Those 60% polyester shirts, valued by traveling evangelists everywhere because they never need to be ironed, not only violate good fashion sense — they also violate the Bible.

☐ *"Six days you shall labor and do all your work. But the seventh day is a Sabbath to the Lord your God; you shall not do any work — you, your son or daughter, your male or female slave, your livestock, or the alien resident in your towns." Exodus 20:9-10*

This is one of the Ten Commandments. Exodus 35:3 elaborates on its meaning by saying, "You shall kindle no fire in all your dwellings on the Sabbath day." To keep this rule faithfully, we would have to do no work on Saturday, the seventh day of the week. However, even if we took interpretive license and applied the rule to Sundays, we still wouldn't be off the hook. Lighting a gas stove to cook dinner or even turning on the lights in our house would violate this rule.

So let's face the facts: No one follows every rule in the Bible. It's not as if the world is divided into those exceptionally holy people who faithfully live out every biblical injunction and the rest of us schmucks who don't. Every reasonable person acknowledges that at least *some* rules in the Bible are inapplicable — which leads to a very important question: When and under what circumstances is it appropriate to depart from a biblical rule?

Some people arbitrarily say the New Testament is binding and the Old Testament is not. But the list we catalogued above includes rules from the New Testament, too. Others make a distinction between "moral" law and "ceremonial" law. They define ceremonial laws as those intended to give Israel an identity distinct from the nations around them. These laws, they say, were for ancient Israel only, and no longer apply. Even if we were to accept this line of thought (which is nowhere mentioned in Scripture), it still begs the question of how to distinguish a ceremonial law from a moral law. Consider, for example, the Sabbath rule, which is one of the Ten Commandments.

It seems disingenuous to argue that one of the Ten Commandments was a mere ceremonial law. Moreover, this line of thought also fails to explain those New Testament rules that are widely disregarded by conservative Christians today.

Is there any consistent, non-arbitrary standard by which we can decide which biblical rules apply and which rules do not? This is a question any thoughtful, honest Christian must confront.

Suppose, for example, there really was a verse in the Bible that prohibited people of the same sex from living in loving, committed relationships. How would we know if we should apply that verse or whether it should fall into the same category as rules about beard-trimming and women being silent? Whose standard of interpretation should we follow? Should we return to Orthodox Judaism and strive to keep every detail of every rule? Should we listen to our favorite televangelist and keep those rules he or she identifies as important? Should we just do whatever feels right? *We think not.*

We who call ourselves Christians confess Jesus as Lord. That means he's the boss. It follows, therefore, that we should use the same approach as Jesus did to decide which Scriptures apply and which do not. Jesus should be our gold standard of biblical interpretation.

With this in mind, let's examine three key instances when Jesus was asked whether he or his disciples should follow a particular scriptural rule. We'll try to identify the standards he used to determine whether and how to apply these biblical rules. As you'll see, Jesus offers us standards which are not arbitrary and which do not rely on fuzzy logic or mere whims.

The common-sense approach to Scripture (Mark 7:14-15)

These verses immediately follow an argument Jesus had with the Scribes and Pharisees (the religious conservatives of his day[2]). In that argument, Jesus criticized the Scribes and Pharisees for allowing legalism to prevail over common sense. The Scribes and Pharisees had apparently concluded that an adult child who pledged his assets to the temple upon his death was thereby relieved of any moral obligation to support his parents during life (even though he could use the assets to support himself). This conclusion was based on the premise that vows to God must never be broken — so a vow pledging assets took precedence over the moral obligation to care for parents.[3] Jesus despised this kind of cold-hearted legalistic reasoning.

Apparently the dialogue with the Scribes and the Pharisees made Jesus so angry he decided the time was right to clearly and unambiguously repudiate legalism.

The text tells us, "he called the crowd to him." (7:14) This was unusual for Jesus — usually the crowds came to him first — but apparently what Jesus wanted to say couldn't wait. So Jesus summoned the crowds. And he said, "Listen to me, all of you, and understand; there is nothing outside the person that by going in can defile, but the things that go out are what defile." (7:14-15) Then he turned and went inside the house. That was it! It seems like a peculiar thing to say. To make sense of it, we need to know a little more about Old Testament law.

The first five books of the Old Testament contain what the Scribes and Pharisees called the Torah, or "Teaching." It is this "Teaching" that contains the 613 rules we mentioned earlier, and the Pharisees, particularly, tried very hard to follow these rules exactly.[4] Remember, among the 613 rules of the Torah there are many that describe which foods are permissible to eat and which are not. Jesus was referring to these rules in his statement. Apparently Jesus seized on these rules as a classic example of legalism.

The food rules, found mostly in Leviticus and Deuteronomy, include long lists of animals. The author puts each animal in a category of "clean" (acceptable for food) or "unclean" (unacceptable for food). In the King James Version of the Bible, the text even uses the word "abomination" (a word people often use against gay, lesbian, and bisexual people) to describe some of the animals.[5] Eating them was deemed an abomination. (Funny how most Christians don't take the word "abomination" quite so seriously when it comes to eating pork.)

Reading the Old Testament from our twenty-first century perspective, we are left to speculate on the rationale for calling some foods clean and others unclean. We can't claim to know what the author of Leviticus was thinking four thousand years ago. However, the conservative *Mercer Bible Dictionary* suggests one plausible explanation for the food rules. In this dictionary's section called *Law In The Old Testament,* it says:

"The rules [about unclean foods] have been explained as early notions of hygiene, as allegories, or simply as preferences of taste; however, their key probably is the one stated with the rules themselves: they are for keeping Israel holy. . . .

Among the animals of Leviticus 11, the unclean are those of mixed or confused identity: if for example birds typically fly and quadrupeds walk, a quadruped that flies — the bat (vs. 19) — is perceived as having a confused identity; it is unclean. The birds listed as unclean (vs. 13-19) swim or dive or in some other way do not behave like birds. . . .

[T]he principle is clear: the animal perceived as 'ordered' has its holiness and is clean; the animal having blurred identity is contaminated and to be avoided. . . ."[6]

The view expressed above represents a growing scholarly consensus — the animals designated as unclean in the Old Testament are those whose behavior departs from what was considered normative for their class.[7] In other words, the distinction between clean and unclean animals was based on the same "creation order" argument often used today against gay, lesbian, and bisexual people.

Today many try to argue that women who love women (or men who love men) are confused and behaving in a way humans are not supposed to. Jesus repudiates this way of thinking in Mark 7:14-15.

The author of Mark tells us that as Jesus walked into the house, his disciples asked for clarification. The principle Jesus had articulated was so breathtaking in its scope (apparently setting aside all the biblical rules on clean foods in one fell swoop), the disciples must have thought they had misunderstood. A little bit annoyed that they still didn't understand, Jesus said, "Do you not see that whatever goes into a person from the outside cannot defile, since it enters not the heart but the stomach, and goes out into the sewer?" The author then adds a parenthetical statement, "Thus he declared all foods clean." (7:18-19)

So, what was the basis of Jesus' decision that the Bible's food laws need not be kept? For those of us who come from conservative backgrounds the answer is shocking. He used common sense. He observed something that all of us recognize as true — externalities don't matter when judging a person's spirit — and then he threw out the rules on clean foods because they go against this common-sense truth. Eating birds that dive doesn't affect a person's soul.

Of course, we all understand this truth without being told. All of us have friends or relatives who don't know how to dress. Maybe it's Great Aunt Ruth, who insists on wearing that red hat with the purple dress. Or Cousin "It," whose hair is completely out of control. Jeff and Tyler both have articles of clothing in their past that they regret. For Jeff it's a blue, clover-leaf patterned shirt he wore with maroon and green plaid hip huggers in the seventies. (He thought all the gals on campus were staring at him because he looked so good!) For Tyler, it's that red, yellow, and blue plaid jacket with the flower buttons, which he insisted was "cool" his junior year of college. We may chuckle at the thought of our friends in their wild clothes, but their bad taste doesn't change the fact that they are good people, with good hearts, whom we trust and love. We know instinctively that externalities don't matter.

When someone says, "Women are supposed to love men; lesbians love women; therefore lesbians are unnatural and unholy," our answer should be the same as Jesus Christ's in the seventh chapter of Mark.

Common sense tells us the physical characteristics (the hair color, the skin color, or the sex) of the person we love have no more effect on our hearts, our souls, or our holiness, than the physical character-istics of what we eat. Yes, being a bad partner in a gay relationship would affect our heart, just as it would affect the heart of someone in a heterosexual relationship. Being unfaithful to our spouse — that too can affect our souls. But the gender — the physical characteristics of the genitals — of the one we love is an outward attribute and inconsequential to our soul's status with God.

This is the principle Jesus summoned the crowd to hear. Jesus looked at the scriptural rules involving food and tested them according to the common-sense understanding that externalities don't affect the soul. By this standard, he determined all foods are clean, despite the objections of religious conservatives who wanted a rigid, legalistic interpretation of Scripture.

By taking the same approach as Jesus, gay people can look directly in the eyes of a conservative Christian who still holds externalities against them, and say, "There is nothing about the outward appearance of who we love that can affect our souls." That is common sense. On the authority of the teachings of Jesus, we can confidently say that even if there were a scriptural rule against loving, committed same-sex relationships (which there is not), it should be set aside under the principles articulated by Jesus in Mark 7.

Beware of any preacher who tells you to check your common sense at the door. Jesus Christ, the Son of God, taught us to use common sense. But he didn't stop there.

The standard of compassion (Matthew 12:7)

In the twelfth chapter of the Gospel of Matthew, Jesus is accused of allowing his disciples to break one of the Ten Commandments. Jesus' response gives further insight into his approach to scriptural rules.

The chapter begins by telling us, "Jesus went through the grainfields on the Sabbath." (Matthew 12:1) While walking in a field, the disciples became hungry and began plucking heads of grain and eating them. Some Pharisees were also in the field, and recognized that picking grain is forbidden by the Old Testament rule against doing work on the Sabbath. They came to Jesus and said, "Look, your disciples are doing what is unlawful on the Sabbath." (Matthew 12:2)

Remember, the Sabbath rule is one of the Ten Commandments. Exodus 20:8-10 clearly states that no work of any kind is to be done on the Sabbath. Exodus 35:6 says even lighting a fire to keep one's house warm is forbidden on the Sabbath. To emphasize how important this rule is, Numbers 15:32-36 tells of a man who was found gathering sticks on the Sabbath. When the people of Israel asked what they should do with the man, Moses told them to stone him to death. And in case someone were to wonder whether picking grain was considered work, Exodus 34:21 specifies, "even in plowing time and in harvest time, you shall rest" on the Sabbath. The disciples of Jesus were clearly acting unlawfully, and if Jesus were a legalist he would have thought, "The Bible says it. I believe it. That settles it." And he would have told his disciples to stop picking grain. But that's not how Jesus responded.

Instead, after making several preliminary points, Jesus went right to the heart of the matter. He said to the Pharisees, "If you had known what this means, 'I desire mercy and not sacrifice,' you would not have condemned the guiltless." (12:7)

Jesus accused the Pharisees of condemning the guiltless, even though his disciples had clearly broken a biblical rule! His response seems improper to those of us from legalistic Christian backgrounds. So we ask, what was the basis for Jesus' position? The answer can be found in the quotation from Hosea 6:6, "I desire mercy and not sacrifice."

Hosea was one of the Old Testament prophets who chastised God's people at a time when they were meticulously following the law, but ignoring the human suffering around them. Amos, who prophesied around the same time as Hosea, talked about how people of the time were attending places of worship, offering sacrifices, and then going home to cheat the poor and foster injustice.[8] Jesus accused the Pharisees of doing the same thing: They were more concerned with rule keeping than with human hunger. Jesus' point is clear: Human need is more important than rules — even rules found in the Bible.

This point is reinforced in the Gospel of Mark's version of this same story. There, Jesus tells the Pharisees, "The Sabbath was made for humankind and not humankind for the Sabbath." (Mark 2:27) To legalists, this is a shocking statement — a loophole big enough to drive a bus through. Jesus seemed to be saying that biblical rules are intended to benefit people and should not be applied when they would have the opposite effect. By so doing, Jesus imposed upon his followers the obligation to evaluate the impact of biblical rules, rather than mindlessly applying them without regard to human need or suffering. That may make us uncomfortable, but remember: Jesus is Lord. If Jesus teaches a more compassionate approach than the preachers and teachers of our day, we need to bow the knee to Jesus.

The record we have of Jesus' life illustrates that Jesus always chose compassion for people over strict adherence to biblical rules. When a person came to Jesus with a sickness, Jesus ignored the rules against work on the Sabbath and healed the person. And he became angry with those who argued that, out of deference to the Sabbath rule, he should delay the healing for one day. (Luke 13:10-17) Once, when a woman was caught in adultery, Jesus ignored the biblical rule that stated she must be stoned, forgave her and prompted her to learn from her mistakes. (John 8:1-11) The law required ceremonial hand washing before every meal, but Jesus ate with people who couldn't afford the extra water required. (Mark 7:1-22) Over and over, Jesus chose people over the rules — compassion over legalism. And he was constantly criticized for it by religious conservatives who believed biblical rules should remain rigid. (Luke 6:7; 11:53-54)

With all of this as background, let's turn again to our subject. Suppose there was a rule in the Bible that prohibited even committed, loving relationships between people of the same sex. How would such a rule fare under the standard of compassion taught by Jesus Christ? Think about that question as you read the following story about a friend of ours:

Her name is Judy Van. She attended a Christian school in Missouri. There she met a friend whom we will call Jill. Judy and Jill sang together in churches, blessing many congregations. They traveled together, ate together, laughed together, and fell in love. Judy says her love for Jill opened a whole new world to her. Until then, she'd always wondered why everyone made such a big deal about romantic love.

These two godly women spent the next few years in school, ministering together, enjoying each other's company, and singing their songs for other Christians. But there was always a conflict in their souls. They feared that perhaps their love was unacceptable to God — after all, that's what they'd always been taught. Finally, it came time to apply to graduate schools. Judy went to one school and Jill went to another.

At her new school, Judy met a self-identified lesbian for the first time. She was amazed to find there were other people with the same feelings, and she was glad to finally have a label for what she had felt for Jill. When she saw Jill again, she said, "Jill, I know what we are! We're lesbians."

Jill was horrified. "You may be a lesbian, but I'm not! Don't ever call me that again."

Judy went on to live as God had created her. She eventually met her spouse, Denise, and together they have become a vital part of God's work at their local church. Over the past few years their lives have had many ups and downs, but they've always had each other to lean on for support and encouragement. Judy says she's found true love and acceptance in Denise, and she's happier than she's ever been.

Unlike Judy, Jill ran from her feelings. She married a man — a Baptist minister — perhaps hoping, like so many gay people before her, that marriage would change her. Years later, Judy saw her at a meeting they both attended. Judy rushed up to Jill to greet her, but Jill could not look her in the eye. "I could see her thinking about what could have been," Judy says. It was a sad, sad moment.

Now, look into your heart. Connect with the Spirit of Jesus Christ, and ask yourself: Would a God of love, who desires mercy more than sacrifice, rather that people live as Judy or as Jill? Don't hide behind legalism. Have the courage to be thoughtful and compassionate, as Jesus taught.

Another Christian friend of ours spent twenty years in public Christian ministry, trying to be straight, before his house of cards fell down around him, and his wife and church threw him out. Is this the life God desires for people? Everyone in that situation — the gay man, his wife, and his children — were deeply hurt because this man had been taught that God wanted him to try to be something he could never be.

We're not talking about the common stereotype of a radical fairy, riding half-naked on the back of a float in some Gay Pride parade, looking for his next sexual conquest. We're talking about ordinary human beings wanting to enter into loving relationships with the blessing of God — for better, for worse, for richer, for poorer, in sickness and in health, 'til death do them part.

When Jeff's spouse, David, was in the hospital with a brain tumor, and David was frightened of what might happen, Jeff slept on the floor of the hospital room for eight days. For Jeff it was no trouble, his only thought was for the one he loved.

When our friend, Rev. Sherry Poepsel, found out her partner Pam was sick with cancer, she immediately disrupted her own schedule and spent months caring for Pam, even though it meant setting the alarm to change Pam's dressings every six hours. Her caring response was immediate and came from a deep and abiding love.

Now, consult the Spirit of Jesus Christ, and answer honestly whether you believe the God who loves mercy and not sacrifice would have preferred that David and Pam had been alone in their illnesses? Some may say, "Well, David and Pam could have been cared for by their extended families." But let's not be trite. We all know the love and companionship of a spouse is unique, and it defies godly compassion to suggest David and Pam should forfeit that special love in order to uphold a pharisaical passion for the sanctity of rules.

Our friend, the Rev. Howard Warren tells of a story that illustrates the results of a system requiring sacrifice and ignoring mercy. When Howard was in seminary, he had a classmate named Troy. One day school authorities discovered Troy was gay and expelled him. Three days later Troy took his own life. The story of Troy's suicide, and the reason for it, was the buzz on campus for weeks. No one would speak openly, but behind closed doors everyone was talking. Anguished by Troy's death, Howard finally raised his hand in class one day, and asked a trusted professor, "What about Troy?" Howard says the professor thought for a moment and then said, "Troy did it for the good of the Church."

Can you feel the white-hot anger of Jesus Christ at such a response? If Jesus had been present in that class, he surely would have said to that professor, "If you had known what this means, 'I desire mercy and not sacrifice,' you would not have condemned the guiltless!" Where did we Christians go wrong? When was it that we started resembling the Pharisees more than the one we call "Lord?"

It's time we Christians had the courage to follow the example of Jesus, who taught that compassion is more important than rules. Even if there *were* a rule in the Bible prohibiting homosexuals from entering into loving, committed relationships with a person of the same sex, we should have the courage to set it aside in the name of Christ, who taught us God desires mercy, not sacrifice.

The responsibility of Jesus' followers (Matthew 17:24-27)

By now, it's obvious Jesus did not approach the Scriptures legalistically. Instead, his ethical decision-making process reflected a dynamic balance between: (1) deep respect for Scripture, and (2) Spirit-led discernment based on compassion and common sense.

A question often arises as people learn about Jesus' non-legalistic approach to Scripture: How do we know Jesus wanted us to approach Scripture the same way? After all, Jesus was the Son of God. When Jesus set aside a rule using the standards of common sense and compassion, he did so with the authority of the Son of God. Surely Jesus doesn't want us, normal humans, presuming to do the same.

It would certainly be easier if we didn't have to pray or think about these difficult and complicated issues. Who wants that kind of moral responsibility? It would be much easier if we could just disengage our hearts and heads and regard the Bible as a book of laws. But Jesus doesn't let us off so easily.

In Matthew 17:24, we're told a temple tax collector came to Simon Peter and said, "Does your teacher not pay the temple tax?" This tax was prescribed in Exodus 30:11-16. It was collected once a year from every Jewish male over the age of twenty and was used to run the temple.[9] Peter assumed Jesus would obey this ancient biblical law, so he told the tax collector that Jesus did pay the tax, even before going to ask Jesus. When he next saw Jesus, Jesus spoke first. In answer to the unasked question running through Peter's mind, Jesus said, "What do you think, Simon? From whom do kings of the earth take toll or tribute? From their children or from others?" (Matthew 17:25)

Simon Peter had assumed the legalistic approach: "Exodus 30 says it. I believe it. That settles it." Jesus wasn't satisfied. He wanted to teach Peter to think more deeply. So instead of feeding Peter the answer, he asked questions. "What do you think?" Peter responded that the rulers of the earth taxed others and not their children. "Then," Jesus said, "the children are free."

Once again Jesus was hammering at the same point made on the other occasions we've discussed. Jesus was saying, "You, Peter, are free from legalism — from spirituality as simple rule-keeping." Jesus expected his followers, relying on the gift of the Holy Spirit, to think for themselves. (See John 16:12-15) We have a moral obligation to think, to reason, and to be guided by the Holy Spirit, even if that leads us occasionally to conclude that a certain rule in the Bible is inapplicable to us as followers of Jesus. The children are free.

We don't mean to give the impression the followers of Jesus should tear through the Bible, willy-nilly, throwing out whole portions of Scripture simply because they aren't convenient. The approach

Jesus took was much more respectful than that. There are dozens of examples in the gospels where Jesus followed biblical rules, and only about ten where he did not.[10] In fact, in the story we just recounted, Jesus ultimately chose to obey the law. He concluded his lesson by telling Peter to pay the tax, so as not to offend the temple tax collectors (a decision based on compassion for the feelings of his contemporaries). But the tax was paid only after Jesus made it clear to Peter that followers of Jesus cannot put their spiritual lives on auto-pilot. We must constantly ask ourselves, "What do you think?"

That conclusion is frightening for those of us from conservative Christian backgrounds. We're used to our pastors or priests telling us what to do. There's comfort and safety in legalism. But if we are to call ourselves Christians, after Jesus Christ, then we must have the courage to follow him, even when his teachings conflict with those of the pastors and teachers of our past. If we don't, then we're not following his example, and we're not worthy of his name.

Taking the Bible seriously

"But," some may object, "if the Bible is not a book of laws, then what is it?" It is the divinely inspired record of God's work. It tells us about Jesus Christ. It offers numerous examples of how God has interacted with our spiritual ancestors. As such, the Bible contains enormous wisdom for us today. We would be fools to ignore it. It's an incredible gift from God to help guide our lives.

But Jesus taught that this inspired record must not be turned into a set of laws, frozen in time. When we do so, we completely close ourselves off from the other great source of guidance promised by God — the Holy Spirit. Jesus himself said he had many things he wanted to teach his disciples that they were not yet ready to hear. But he promised they (and we) would receive the gift of the Holy Spirit, who would guide them (and us) into all truth. (John 16:12-15) Here, then, is Jesus' formula for finding truth: The ancient Scriptures must be balanced with the dynamic real-time work of the Holy Spirit. As Jesus said in Matthew 13:52, "Every scribe who has been trained in the kingdom of heaven [*i.e.*, every person committed to the teachings of Jesus] is like the master of a household who brings out of his treasure what is new and what is old." True followers of Christ respect the "old" (*i.e.*, the ancient Scriptures), but we are also not afraid to bring forth what is new.

The ultimate irony is that we who have been set free from legalism are so very tempted to return to it. The New Testament has a lot to say about this. In fact, two whole books of the New Testament (Romans and Galatians) are devoted largely to warning us not to retreat into legalism. Listen to what Paul says in Galatians 5:1 and following:

> "For freedom Christ has set us free. Stand firm, therefore, and do not submit again to a yoke of slavery. Listen! I, Paul, am telling you that if you let yourselves be circumcised [symbolic of returning to legalism], Christ will be of no benefit to you. . . . You who want to be justified by the law have cut yourselves off from Christ; you have fallen away from grace."

Paul, who fought so vigorously against the legalistic tendencies of some early Christians, would be horrified at the sight of so many modern Christians determined to turn his own writings into a "new Mosaic Law" for Christians.

Some may object that if the Scriptures are not applied as laws, people will have license to do anything they want. Paul's opponents feared the same thing. (Romans 6:1, 15) But this objection ignores the presence of the Holy Spirit. Paul was confident that the guidance of the Holy Spirit would be sufficient to prevent sincere believers from error. "If you are led by the Spirit," he said, "you are not subject to the law." (Galatians 5:18) We who follow Jesus must be open to both the old and the new (both Scripture and Spirit) working in dynamic combination. This is how a follower of Jesus discerns truth.

Freedom in Christ

So we return, once again, to the question: What if there were a rule in the Bible which prohibited loving, committed relationships between people of the same sex? As chapters one and two make clear, there is no such rule, but suppose there was. Would that rule apply to the lives of gay, lesbian, and bisexual Christians today?

If such a rule existed, on the authority of Jesus Christ that rule should be set aside, in the same way, and for the same reasons, as Jesus boldly set aside several other biblical rules. Common sense tells us the gender of our spouse is an incidental characteristic that has no impact on our holiness. Compassion compels us to stop the enormous pain inflicted on gay people by the Church when it insists they deny who God created them to be.

If you want to be trapped in an ugly spirit that says externalities are more important than souls, that says rules are more important than people, then go ahead. But that is the spirit of the enemies of Jesus Christ. The Jesus of history fought against the tyranny of legalism. The Jesus of history taught us to think. The Jesus of history said, "The children are free."

So, the scholars can debate the meaning of obscure Scripture passages until the cows come home. In the final analysis, the outcome of this debate on homosexuality and the Bible turns not on any one, two, or three specific passages, but rather on the fundamental, overarching biblical principles of compassion and common sense — principles that are not subject to cultural tides or the pendulum swings of scholarship. If the world's five greatest Bible scholars were to come forward tomorrow and declare that Romans 1 really does, in their opinion, prohibit loving gay relationships, then, on the authority of Jesus Christ, we would place that rule in the same category as rules about beard-trimming and the silence of women in the church. Legalists can howl and scream all they want, just as Jesus' opponents used to do. We don't care. We are God's children. We are free.

Notes

1   *Jewish Literacy: The Most Important Things to Know about the Jewish Religion, Its People and Its History* (W. Morrow, New York, 1991) by Rabbi Joseph Telushkin covers the 613 *Mitzvot* (as the commandments are called in Hebrew) on pages 495-496, and in the chapter that follows.

2   *The Encyclopedia to the Master Study Bible* published as part of the *New American Standard Master Study Bible* (Holman Bible Publishers, Nashville, 1981) includes an excellent section on "Jewish Sects and Orders" on pages 1960-1971. It states that the Pharisees as a group were committed to keeping their religion pure by strictly following the traditions which had been handed down to them. Unfortunately, it was their insistence on traditional interpretations which made it so hard for them to accept Jesus.

3   *The Interpreter's Bible*, Vol. 7 (Abingdon Press, Nashville, 1982), pages 750-751.

4   Again, see *Jewish Literacy* and the *Encyclopedia to the Master Study Bible*. On page 1964, the Encyclopedia states the Pharisees intended to " 'fence the law,' or to lesson the risk of breaking it" by building around it a "multiplicity of subtle distinctions and vexatious rules," which resulted in "an oppression to the conscience" rather than the desired effect of strengthening God's word. Does this attitude sound familiar?

5   The list of animals called "abominations" is found in Leviticus 11.

6   *Mercer Dictionary of the Bible* (Mercer University Press, Macon, GA, 1990), page 505.

7   F. Scott Spencer, *The Ethiopian Eunuch and His Bible* (Source: *Biblical Theology Bulletin*, vol. 22, no. 4), page 159 and sources cited there.

8   See the introductions to Hosea and Amos in *The New Oxford Annotated Bible* (Oxford University Press, New York, 1994).

9   See the *The New Oxford Annotated Bible* notes to Matthew 17:24-27. The *Harper Collins Bible Dictionary* (HarperSanFrancisco, 1996) also states, on page 699, "this tax was collected in the month preceding Passover and had to be paid with a special silver coin from Tyre."

10 Other instances where Jesus departed from biblical rules include the following: Matthew 5:27-42; 12:9-13; 19:1-12; Mark 3:1-5; Luke 6:6-12; 13:10-17; 14:1-6; and John 8:1-11.

Chapter Four

Relearning an Ancient Lesson

In chapter three, we studied Jesus' dynamic, non-legalistic approach to Scripture, and we saw how he expected his followers to approach Scripture in the same way. Not long after Jesus' departure, his earliest followers were put to the test. An influx of new Christians with a different lifestyle created tension in the Church and raised difficult biblical questions. Would Church leaders have the courage to follow in Jesus' footsteps and interpret Scripture based on compassion and common sense, or would they snap back to safe, spiritless legalism? The story of this struggle is told in the New Testament book of Acts.

Setting the stage: Jewish and Gentile Christians

Virtually all Jesus' earliest followers came from Jewish backgrounds and, even after placing faith in Christ, continued to observe the Law of Moses as set forth in the first five books of the Bible. This meant (among other things) they ate only food designated as "clean" in Leviticus and Deuteronomy. They also circumcised their male children as God commanded Abraham to do in Genesis 17:11-14.

Early in the book of Acts, Christians had not yet drawn the conclusion that "Jesus declared all foods clean." (Mark 7:19) Mark's Gospel had not yet been written,[1] and Christians were still wrestling with the more daring aspects of Jesus' teachings. In the meantime, they continued living as they always had, eating kosher (according to biblical law) and keeping other aspects of the Law of Moses — after all, this was part of Scripture.

But as the good news of Jesus began to spread, many non-Jews (often called "Gentiles") began to accept Christ. Unlike their Jewish counterparts, Gentiles had not grown up keeping the Law of Moses.

They found it difficult to understand and follow all the intricacies of the Law, and many of them simply refused. Perhaps they instinctively understood what Jesus had taught — that rules about food, clothing, shaving beards, and so forth don't have any bearing on the soul. At any rate, they did not keep the Law of Moses, creating an enormous dilemma for the Jewish Christians who believed the biblical laws were binding. Jewish Christians, who held all the prominent positions in the Church, wondered what should be done about these Gentiles who claimed to believe in Jesus, but lived a lifestyle at odds with Scripture.

Thankfully, the early Church did not break apart, but used this challenge as an opportunity to grow their faith. We in the modern Church can learn much from their example, for the question they faced (what to do with Gentile believers) bears a striking resemblance to the question we face (what to do with gay and lesbian believers).

Scene 1: Peter and Cornelius (Acts 10)

In Acts 10 we're told the Apostle Peter was praying on the roof of his house one day when he became hungry and fell into a trance. While in the trance, Peter saw heaven open and a large sheet, lowered by its four corners, descend to where he could reach it. The sheet was filled with all kinds of unclean animals — animals considered unfit for food under the Law of Moses. As Peter watched the animals descend, a voice said, "Get up, Peter; kill and eat." (Acts 10:13) Peter was horrified. He assumed it was the voice of God he heard, but the voice was telling him to violate Scripture.

So, Peter refused, "By no means, Lord; for I have never eaten anything that is profane or unclean." (Acts 10:14)

The voice thundered back, "What God has made clean, you must not call profane!" (Acts 10:15) Twice more Peter refused. And twice more the voice told him not to call profane what God had made clean.

After he came out of the trance, as Peter was struggling with the meaning of his vision, three men came to the door and told him a Roman centurion named Cornelius had sent them to bring him to the centurion's house. God told Peter he should go with these men without hesitation, so he did.

From our perspective in the twenty-first century, it might be easy to miss the amazing aspects of this story. But, thankfully, the author of Acts knew his audience would be non-Jewish[2], so he recorded Peter's explanation of what he'd learned. At Cornelius's house, Peter began by saying, "You yourselves know that it is unlawful for a Jew to associate with or to visit a Gentile, but God has shown me that I should not call anyone profane or unclean." (Acts 10:28) Prompted by his vision, Peter had begun to rethink his views, and had opened his heart and mind to the possibility that people who didn't live exactly as he did might also be acceptable to God.

Then, the story tells us, an amazing thing happened. As Peter preached to these Gentiles about Jesus, "the Holy Spirit fell upon all who heard the word." (Acts 10:44) And the strict Jewish believers who'd come with Peter "were astounded that the gift of the Holy Spirit had been poured out even on the Gentiles." (Acts 10:45) They were amazed that God's presence could dwell in people who were violating so many scriptural rules. But Peter, with his new perspective, said, "Can anyone withhold the water for baptizing these people who received the Holy Spirit just as we have?" (Acts 10:47) He remembered how God had told him not to call profane anything (or anyone) God had made clean, so he ordered these Gentiles baptized, thereby accepting them as equal members of the Church.

Unfortunately, this isn't the end of the story. It would be years before the early Church finally put to rest the question of what to do with Gentile Christians. In fact, in the very next chapter of Acts, we find Peter forced to defend his actions against the attacks of legalistic Christians in Jerusalem. They demanded to know why he would go to the house of a Gentile and eat there when the Bible strictly forbade it. (Acts 11:3) Peter told them everything that had happened leading up to his visit with Cornelius, and concluded by saying, "If God gave them the same gift that was given to us when we believed in the Lord Jesus Christ, who was I that I could hinder God?" (Acts 11:17) When Peter's critics heard this, the text says they were "silenced" and stated with amazement, "Then God has given even to the Gentiles the repentance that leads to life." (Acts 11:18) At least for the time being, the legalistic Christians had to admit God wanted Gentile Christians in the community.

Like many Christians today, the legalists of Acts were initially willing to accept people who didn't follow Scripture the way they saw fit. However, many of them soon wanted to put stipulations on their acceptance. Perhaps it was okay for these Gentile Christians to receive the Holy Spirit and be baptized into the Christian community, but once they were baptized, it seems, there were certain standards of living that some believed had to be followed. Those standards, the legalists thought, should be determined by a close reading of the Mosaic Law. After all, they knew best. They were the older Christians, they were the ones in authority, and they knew the proper way to read the Bible. Although legalistic Christians had lost the first battle, they weren't about to give up.

Scene 2: The showdown (Acts 15)

Around this time, the Apostle Paul began to rise to prominence as a Christian missionary to the Gentiles. His work began in the city of Antioch, located several hundred miles north of Jerusalem — a long way off at a time when most people walked everywhere. While the church in Jerusalem was still flirting with legalism, Paul enthusiastically embraced a non-legalistic approach to faith and Scripture. Under his leadership, Gentiles were flocking into the church at Antioch. Worse yet (from a legalist's perspective), the church at Antioch commissioned missionaries, and began spreading their message to other cities.

Legalist Christians in Jerusalem were alarmed. Too many people were getting the idea they could become Christians without following the Law of Moses. It seemed as if Scripture was being watered down to appeal to as many as possible. So, they sent their own missionaries to Antioch to warn the Gentile believers. Their message was blunt, "Unless your are circumcised according to the custom of Moses, you cannot be saved." (Acts 15:1) They wanted the Gentile Christians to understand the importance of the biblical laws.

Two camps soon arose in the Antioch church. One group sided with Paul and taught that Gentile Christians need not follow the Law of Moses. The other group sided with the legalists and insisted that every aspect of the Law still applied. The dissention became so vigorous it threatened to destroy the Antioch church. To resolve the dispute, they sent a delegation to Jerusalem to seek an official ruling from the apostles and elders who still lived there. This meeting, recorded in Acts Chapter 15, is often called the "Jerusalem Council."

We don't know how long the Jerusalem Council lasted, because the author of Acts only tells us what happened near the end of the meeting. The author says "after there had been much debate," Peter stood to speak. (Acts 15:7) He reminded everyone of his experience with Cornelius and with other early Gentile converts. He reminded them how God, who knows everything about everyone, had given these people the Holy Spirit "just as God has given us." (Acts 15:8)

"God has made no distinction between them and us," Peter said. (Acts 15:9) And then he made an appeal based on compassion, asking the Council to set aside their legalistic reading of Scripture. "Now, therefore," he pleaded, "why are you putting God to the test by placing on the neck of the disciples a yoke that neither our ancestors nor we have been able to bear?" (Acts 15:10) He didn't try to use Scripture to argue against their reading of the Law of Moses; he simply pointed out that even the legalists couldn't keep track of and follow every one of the 613 rules. So, how could they expect these Gentile converts to do what they themselves found impossible? It was a matter of compassion.

Next Paul and Barnabas spoke, sharing "all the signs and wonders that God had done through them among the Gentiles." (Acts 15:12) Again, their argument wasn't based on a nuanced interpretation of Scripture. It was an argument of common sense: If God is doing all these great miracles and transforming lives within the Gentile community, then how are we to argue against that?

Finally James stood up to speak. James was the brother of Jesus and the most important leader in the Jerusalem church. He was also one of the more legalistic Jewish Christians.[3] But he had been listening carefully, and with an open heart. He first reminded the Council of what Peter had said. Then he showed how Peter's experiences fit nicely with his interpretation of some of the Hebrew prophets. He quoted Amos, Jeremiah, and Isaiah, using them in a way that would make sense to a first-century Jewish audience. Finally, he stated his own opinion, "we should not trouble those Gentiles who are turning to God." (Acts 15:19) Instead, James recommended the Council simply ask Gentiles to abstain from several practices especially offensive to Jewish Christians.[4] He suggested they be asked to abstain from eating food previously offered to idols. And he asked that they abstain from fornication, from eating animals killed by strangulation, and from eating blood. (Acts 15:20)

The Greek word translated "fornication" here is *porneia.* It refers primarily to prostitution, including temple prostitution, but also can be used when referring to sexual immorality in general.[5] Thus, the Gentiles were being instructed to abstain from any sexual immorality — that is, any sexual activity prohibited by Scripture. As shown in the first three chapters of this book, this would include various forms of promiscuous and idolatrous homosexual sex, but not committed, loving gay relationships (which are affirmed by Scripture).

The reference to animals killed by strangulation is a little less clear. It probably refers to animals who were killed in such a way that their blood remained in the meat. Meat killed in this way was a delicacy to the Greeks and Romans, but was particularly repugnant to Jews.[6]

The apostles and elders in Jerusalem agreed with James's recommendation, and sent emissaries to Antioch to share the good news. They wrote a letter to the Christians "of Gentile origin" in Antioch, welcoming them into the Church and asking only that they follow the short list of rules James had recommended. It was a stunning defeat for legalism.

You will know them by their fruits.

As we evaluate the implications of the decision of the Jerusalem Council, it is important to note that both Peter and Paul presented very similar arguments. Neither is said to have made a biblical textual argument. Instead, both gave eyewitness testimony to the presence of God's Spirit among the Gentiles. As the old saying goes, "Seeing is believing." Peter and Paul knew what they had seen; the Gentile believers were just as full of the grace, love, and power of the Holy Spirit as Jewish Christians. For Peter and Paul, this was conclusive. Why put God to the test?

Peter and Paul were simply applying a principle Jesus himself had articulated. In the Sermon on the Mount, Jesus said, "By their fruits you will know them," and "A good tree cannot bear bad fruit, nor can a bad tree bear good fruit." (Matthew 7:16, 18) The leaders of the early Church, recognizing the validity of this standard, humbly yielded, even though accepting the Gentiles was counterintuitive and contrary to how they had interpreted Scripture.

Gay, lesbian, and bisexual Christians ask nothing more than that they be judged by the same biblical standard. Following the example of Peter and Paul, we (the authors) share what we have observed among the modern Gentiles — gay, lesbian, and bisexual Christians.

Consider Sarah Fershee. Sarah radiates warmth, love, peace, and joy like few you will ever meet. Sensing the presence of the peace of Christ, strangers instantly feel comfortable around her; they open up and share their troubles. But it wasn't always so. As a teenager and young adult, Sarah suffered from profound mental illness brought on by childhood tragedies. At age 17, she was institutionalized, depressed and listless. The doctors told her parents that shock treatments were the only solution. She endured 69 shock treatments over a six month period to no avail. By now, she was being fed intravenously. Doctors told her parents that her systems were shutting down and she would probably die. If she survived, the doctors said it was likely she would always be institutionalized.

Desperate, her parents took Sarah to another facility — a Christian hospital, where she received a combination of quality psychotherapy and prayerful support. There, she began a decades long healing process. If you were to meet Sarah today, you would never guess she once had struggled so profoundly. She exudes serenity.

Sarah attributes her healing to many influences: a supportive Christian community, a therapist who was both professionally qualified and spiritually attuned, books, prayer partners, and the prayers of many. But beyond that, Sarah says, "there has definitely been for years the sense that I'm traveling alongside Jesus — my healer, my teacher, my brother, my savior." Like Mary Magdalene in the Gospels, Sarah has been healed, and now radiates the love of God to all around her. The fact that Sarah is a lesbian is no impediment. God is working through her mightily.

Mike Driskell first learned about Jesus in both fundamentalist Baptist and charismatic Christian circles. When he came out, he was no longer welcome. But Christ is still the center of Mike's life. Once, Mike's beloved dog Isaiah slipped his collar and chain and got hit by a car. X-rays taken by the vet showed a complete break in one of Isaiah's hind legs. The vet said surgery was the only way Isaiah could ever regain use of the leg, but Mike didn't have the $400 necessary for the surgery. On the way home from the vet and again that evening, Mike wept and prayed for a miracle. A friend of Mike's came over to the house and together they laid hands on Isaiah and "agreed" in prayer. Within a week, Isaiah was running and romping, making full use of his leg. No further treatment was required. Since that time, God has used Mike in other miraculous healings.

David Squire, too, was raised in conservative Christian circles. Even though his parents and childhood church believe his homosexuality is a terrible sin, David has never wavered in his belief that he is God's child. David found another church where he is welcomed. A few years ago, David decided to take a big step of faith and follow God's call into ministry. He quit his job as a communications specialist and began working for his church for free. He worked without pay for a full year until his church could begin paying him a meager salary — barely half what he once made.

When you first meet Brenda Wilhelm, her most striking feature is infectious joy. But Brenda hasn't had it easy. Her mother was diagnosed with a degenerative disease. When she became too ill to live on her own, Brenda moved into her home to care for her. It didn't matter to her mother that Brenda is a lesbian. With a grace that can only come from God, Brenda patiently nurtured her mother for four and a half years until her death. All who observed Brenda were amazed that she never seemed to grow weary in providing care.

Jesus said, "By their fruits you will know them." Paul carried this further, specifying exactly what we should look for when seeking evidence of the presence of the Holy Spirit. "The fruit of the Spirit is love, joy, peace, patience, kindness, generosity, faithfulness, gentleness, and self-control." (Galatians 5:22) This is precisely what can be seen in abundance in the lives of Sarah, Mike, David, Brenda, and thousands more gay, lesbian, and bisexual Christians.

Beyond this, powerful evidence of the Holy Spirit at work can be seen in entire Christian communities composed predominantly of gay, lesbian, and bisexual believers. For example, we are both part of Jesus Metropolitan Community Church (Jesus MCC) in Indianapolis, Indiana. Jeff is pastor, and Tyler is an active member. When talking with Christians who are skeptical, we often issue a simple challenge: "Worship with us just once, and see if you don't experience the presence of the Holy Spirit among us."

When we join in worship at Jesus MCC, singing praises to God, some raise their hands, some quietly bow their heads, some weep, and some flash radiant smiles, but all sense the profound presence of Christ. Visitors are often deeply moved by their experience. For example, a pastor in the Christian Church (Disciples of Christ), Rev. Linda Patrick, worshiped with us for a period of months while on sabbatical. Noticing that she had been missing from worship services in her own denomination, a theologian friend made inquiry. In her reply, she told her friend what she had experienced among us. Here is her description of holy communion and the worship service:

> "As communion proceeds, the community sings, Taizé-
> style, the old spirituals of the faith which so many of the folk
> lost when they were dis-fellowshiped from their congrega-
> tions of origin. This Sunday we sang, 'Earnestly, tenderly,
> Jesus is calling; calling for you and for me. Come home; come
> home; ye who are weary come home.' As I watched the exiled
> move confidently toward the Table spread, some holding
> hands with partners and friends, some single, heads held
> high, even this ol' singer was silenced by the deafening sounds
> of grace all 'round about me.
>
> "To worship each Sunday in a congregation of more than
> 200 adults, average age 35 (instead of 60!), over half of whom
> are men (who SING!), and lots of kids and every race repre-
> sented, and folk from the hearing and non-hearing world — is
> almost more than I could have hoped for this side of the
> crystal fountain. A dyed in the wool Disciple, I admit that I
> wish it were Disciple. But it's not. It is, however, most assur-
> edly Church and I am blessed, visiting and worshiping there."

Rev. Patrick's experience is reminiscent of that of Peter and his
friends in Cornelius' home. How surprising — and how beautiful —
when Christ is found among those thought to be beyond God's grace.

Most of those who worship in our church are gay and lesbian
people returning to their faith after being shown the door by the
churches in which they were raised. But many others are coming to
faith in Christ for the first time, and giving public profession to that
faith through Christian baptism.

Our church is full of people seeking to learn about Jesus Christ
and grow in their discipleship. We offer multiple weekly Bible studies,
a long-term Discipleship Training track, and many opportunities for
Christian service, ranging from helping the homeless, to caring for
those in nursing homes, to sharing the Gospel, to advocating justice

in the finest tradition of the biblical prophets. Our quest is to be more like Jesus at work, in our relationships, around our children, and in our everyday lives.

And our congregation is not unique. We are only one of *many* gay and lesbian Christian congregations around the world where God's Spirit is moving — not to mention the thousands of gay, lesbian, and bisexual Christians who remain as witnesses to the power of the Holy Spirit in their home churches. Everywhere you look, the gift of the Holy Spirit (God's seal of approval) is evident in the lives of gay and lesbian Christians and our worship communities. "By their fruits you will know them."

Will today's Church leaders, like the apostles and elders at the Jerusalem Council, have the courage and humility to acknowledge what God is doing? Or will they, like so many legalists throughout the history of the Church, work to stifle the moving of the Holy Spirit? We believe the choice is clear — but not easy.

Two steps forward, one step back

Change has always been difficult. Even after the Jerusalem Council, the debate among the early Christians continued. The letter the Jerusalem Council drafted was addressed to those "of Gentile origin." Many legalists seized on this technicality, arguing that it was fine for Christians "of Gentile origin" to not follow the Law of Moses, but Jewish-born Christians must still do so. This led to new struggles between Paul (a Jewish-born Christian who refused legalism) and the Jerusalem legalists. It led to Paul's eventual arrest at the temple, where he was performing purification rituals in an attempt to make himself acceptable to the legalists. (Acts 21:17-36) And it led to a shouting match between Peter and Paul, recorded in Galatians 2:11-14. Apparently even Peter went through a period of waffling back and forth on this issue.

This struggle with legalism has continued throughout the history of the Church. In the Middle Ages, many Christians believed non-Christians should be tortured until they professed faith in Christ and killed if they did not. These torturers cited Scripture, which they interpreted as endorsing this approach. Compassion and common sense tell us they were wrong. Today no self-respecting Christian would defend the practice.

In the 1800s, many in the Church defended slavery, citing Bible passages to justify what they knew in their hearts should be condemned. Their interpretation of certain New Testament passages eased their consciences as they allowed injustice to prevail. Compassion and common sense tell us they were wrong. Today no self-respecting Christian would take this position.

In the late 1800s and early 1900s, many in the Church were opposed to giving women the right to vote. They cited Bible passages, which they interpreted as teaching that women must be subordinate to men, while ignoring the witness of the Holy Spirit and the biblical examples of women who held prominent leadership roles. In their blind opposition to common sense and to the Holy Spirit, they were wrong. Today no self-respecting Christian would take this position.

A few years later, many Christians vigorously opposed the growing phenomenon of female preachers, citing Bible passages they interpreted as prohibiting female leadership in the Church, while ignoring those passages that affirm it. They took their position against female pastors despite the fact that they must have personally encountered women who were just as Spirit-filled as men. The Holy Spirit was showing they were wrong. And today most Christian churches welcome women into ministry of all kinds.

Now the Church faces the question of gay, lesbian, and bisexual Christians. And, true to form, many resist. This isn't new — the pull of legalism has always been strong. In Acts 7:51-52, Stephen spoke words to the legalistic Pharisees that could just as easily be spoken to Christian legalists today:

> "You stiff-necked people, uncircumcised in heart and ears, you are forever opposing the Holy Spirit, just as your ancestors used to do." (Acts 7:51)

In today's Church, God needs people with the courage of Paul (and Jesus!), who will stand up against legalists even when that is unpopular. Christians everywhere, in local churches and denominational councils, need to stand up and be counted. This generation of believers faces the same test as many previous generations. If we get it wrong, we will quench the work of the Holy Spirit. If we get it right, we will prove once again, like that first generation of Christians, that God's grace breaks through every prejudice.

In chapters one and two we saw that the Scriptures affirm loving committed same-sex relationships. In chapter three, we saw that compassion and common sense strongly reinforce this conclusion. To this, we now add the witness of the Holy Spirit bearing fruit in the lives of a multitude of gay, lesbian, and bisexual Christians. It's time, once again, for the legalists to step aside and allow God to work.

Notes

1   Most scholars believe Mark wrote his Gospel years after the events described in the book of Acts. By that time, Christians had the advantage of several decades to ponder the full implications of Jesus' teachings. In Acts, we have a record of how the early Church came to understand those implications.

2   The book of Acts is addressed to Theophilus, a Greek word meaning "lover of God." The *New Oxford Annotated Bible* says this might have been a Roman official or any reader who loves God (page 161). However, the Greek name, and the author's penchant for explaining Jewish phrases and laws, implies the audience was non-Jewish.

3   For a good overview of the politics of the Jerusalem church, see *The Story of Christianity, Volume 1* by Justo Gonzalez (HarperSanFrancisco, 1984) pages 18-22. The book of Acts makes James' legalistic tendencies clear, but we also have the New Testament book of James, which was attributed to this Apostle and was likely written by one of his followers (if not by him). That New Testament book, written in a style similar to Proverbs, shows a great respect for the Hebrew Scriptures, with an emphasis on living a holy life guided by the Law of Moses.

4   *The Interpreter's Bible, Volume IX,* pages 205-206.

5   *The Interpreter's Bible, Volume IX* (Abingdon Press, Nashville, 1987) pages 205-206.

6   *The New Oxford Annotated Bible,* page 183NT. And, *The Interpreter's Bible, Volume IX,* pages 205-206. This list of things from which to abstain also bears a striking resemblance to a list which Jewish Rabbis referred to as the "Laws of Noah" or "Noachian Precepts." These were laws supposedly given by God to Noah's sons, and therefore thought to be binding on every righteous person — Jewish and non-Jewish alike. For more on these laws, see Philip Birnbaum's *The Encyclopedia of Jewish Concepts* (Hebrew Publishing Company, New York, 1979), pages 92-93, or Telushkin, pages 509-510.

A Final Word:

To Gay, Lesbian, and Bisexual People

In these last few pages, we would like to speak directly to gay, lesbian, and bisexual people who have experienced rejection by the Church.

As we've already mentioned, Tyler's parents are missionaries. At age twelve, when Tyler first came back to the United States, he hadn't played any team sports. All he knew about football was that the ball was shaped something like an egg. He knew even less about basketball and baseball. He remembers many days during his seventh-grade year when he sat on the bench in P.E. class while students picked teams. Usually the coach would choose two tanned and athletic boys as team captains. Then, those two handsome lads would take turns choosing their teammates. Quickly, the best players stood as their names were called. Then the captains began to put more thought into each decision, as they balanced the pros and cons of picking between the mediocre athletes. Finally, there would only be Tyler and one other child, the smallest in the class. Even then, the team that took Tyler knew they'd gotten the worse player.

Tyler's eighth-grade coach didn't use this barbaric technique for choosing teams, but by then Tyler had already been told too many times that athletic teams didn't want him. So, he decided he didn't want to play team sports. To this day, Tyler doesn't like any team sport. When he does exercise, he prefers activities like climbing and hiking, and cringes at even the thought of a friendly game of volleyball.

Unfortunately, too many of our gay, lesbian, and bisexual sisters and brothers feel the same way about the Christian Church. For years they've been told Jesus doesn't want them on his team. They've experienced pain and embarrassment. And, like Tyler who decided to find alternative athletic activities, they've decided to look elsewhere for spiritual sustenance. Our people have turned in vast numbers to Wicca and other earth religions. They have dabbled in spirituality, leaving group-focused religion for individual spiritual paths. But, more often than not, they've simply given up on their spiritual life and stopped working their spiritual muscles.

If this is where you find yourself, we understand. We've been there, too. But we've learned we must not confuse the negative voices of those who have condemned us with the loving voice of the Jesus of history, who (as we have seen) welcomes us with open arms.

The first two chapters of this book tear down the myth that God doesn't want gay, lesbian, and bisexual people — we are all chosen! Jesus wants *you* on his team. But, being a member of Jesus' team also means working your spiritual muscles. That's one of the lessons of chapters three and four.

We believe Jesus is "the way, the truth, and the life." (John 14:6) In him, we have found abundant life. We are proud to be called his followers, for, as this book has shown, Jesus was not some finger-wagging, hidebound, fun-hating nag — like so many religious leaders seem to become. Jesus was full of life, hope, and grace. He pushed the envelope; he took radical positions. He valued compassion over rules. He was willing to befriend those despised by good religious people in his day. Jesus made a point of reaching out to Samaritans, a despised ethnic and religious minority and to women. (Luke 10:25-37; John 4:1-42) In a sharp break with religious practices in his day, Jesus welcomed female disciples. (Luke 8:1-3; 10:38-42) Jesus shared meals with tax collectors, prostitutes, and sinners. (Luke 7:36-50; 15:1-2; 19:1-10) And, as we have seen, Jesus affirmed a gay soldier who sought healing for his male lover. (Matthew 8:5-13)

We invite you to rediscover the real Jesus.

If this is the first time you've thought about what it means to be a follower of Jesus, or if you're coming back to faith after a long absence, there are a few practices we recommend. First, begin to read the Bible and study what it *does* say. You can start with one of the Gospels (the first four books of the New Testament). If that seems too difficult, see if you can find some good books on the Bible that will help you think about what it means for you to follow Jesus. But beware. The teachings of Jesus are radical. Following him may require some profound changes in key aspects of life (for example, our thought life, our sexual conduct, how we spend our money, and how we treat our enemies), but only you, in dialogue with God, can decide exactly what is required of you. Jesus wants you to think for yourself, and studying the Gospels is a good place to start that process.

Second, find some people who can support you in your faith journey. There are now many gay-affirming Christian churches. Some of the easiest to recognize are the Metropolitan Community Churches, which were started by gays and lesbians, but some Methodist, Episcopal, Presbyterian, United Church of Christ, Disciples, and even Baptist churches are now gay-affirming. You can often find churches listed in gay newspapers, or by asking your friends where they go. You might be surprised how many of your friends go to church!

Finally, ask God to help you on your journey. Jesus taught us that God is a loving parent who will give us what we need. All we have to do is ask. (Matthew 7:7-11) Remember that God loves you and wants what's best for you. God bless you on your journey.

We'll see you in Heaven — let's meet beneath the rainbow that stretches over the throne of God! (Revelation 4:1-3)